THE ANNOTATED SHAKESPEARE

Henry the Fourth, Part One

William Shakespeare

Fully annotated, with an Introduction, by Burton Raffel

With an essay by Harold Bloom

THE ANNOTATED SHAKESPEARE

Yale University Press • *New Haven and London*

Published with assistance from the Mary Cady Tew Memorial Fund.

Designed by Rebecca Gibb.
Set in Bembo type by The Composing Room of Michigan, Inc.
Printed in the United States of America by R. R. Donnelley & Sons.

Library of Congress Cataloging-in-Publication Information
Shakespeare, William, 1564–1616.
Henry the Fourth, part one / William Shakespeare; fully annotated
with an introduction by Burton Raffel; with an essay by Harold Bloom.
p.   cm.—(The annotated Shakespeare)
Includes bibliographical references.
ISBN-13: 978-0-300-10815-6 (pbk.)
ISBN-10: 0-300-10815-X (pbk.)
1. Henry IV, King of England, 1367–1413—Drama.   2. Great Britain—
History—Henry IV, 1399–1413—Drama.   I. Raffel, Burton.
II. Bloom, Harold.   III. Title.
PR2810.A2R34 2006
822.3'3—dc22
2005029100

A catalogue record for this book is available from the British Library.

10 9 8 7 6 5 4 3 2 1

For Clay and Linda Allen

CONTENTS

ABOUT THIS BOOK

In act 2, scene 1, we meet a pair of characters who have no individual names. We see one of them at single point, later in the play, but he has almost nothing to say, there. The other character completely disappears from the play.

AN INNYARD

ENTER A CARRIER WITH A LANTERN IN HIS HAND

Carrier 1 Heigh ho. An it be not four by the day, I'll be hanged. Charles' wain is over the new chimney, and yet our horse not packed. What, Ostler!

Ostler (within) Anon, anon.

Carrier 1 I prithee, Tom, beat Cut's saddle, put a few flocks in the point. The poor jade is wrung in the withers, out of all cess.

ENTER CARRIER 2

Carrier 2 Peas and beans are as dank here as a dog, and that is the next way to give poor jades the bots. This house is turned upside down since Robin Ostler died.

Carrier 1 Poor fellow never joyed since the price of oats rose, it was the death of him.

Carrier 2 I think this be the most villainous house in all London road for fleas. I am stung like a tench.

Carrier 1 Like a tench! By the mass there is ne'er a king in Christendom could be better bit than I have been since the first cock.

Carrier 2 Why, they will allow us ne'er a jordan, and then we leak in your chimney, and your chamber-lye breeds fleas like a loach.

Carrier 1 What, Ostler! Come away and be hanged, come away!

Carrier 2 I have a gammon of bacon, and two razes of ginger, to be delivered as far as Charing Cross.

Carrier 1 God's body, the turkeys in my pannier are quite starved. What, Ostler? A plague on thee, hast thou never an eye in thy head? Canst not hear? And t'were not as good deed as drink, to break the pate on thee, I am a very villain. Come and be hanged! Hast no faith in thee?

This was perfectly understandable, we must assume, to the mostly very average persons who paid to watch Elizabethan plays. But who today can make much sense of it? In this very fully annotated edition, I therefore present this passage, not in the bare form quoted above, but thoroughly supported by bottom-of-the-page notes:

AN INNYARD
ENTER A CARRIER[1] WITH A LANTERN IN HIS HAND

Carrier 1 Heigh ho. An it be not four by the day,[2] I'll be hanged. Charles' wain[3] is over the new chimney, and yet our horse not

---

1 teamster
2 *by the day* = in the morning
3 group of seven bright stars in the Great Bear constellation (wain = chariot, wagon)

packed.[4] What, Ostler![5]

Ostler (*within*) Anon,[6] anon.

Carrier 1 I prithee, Tom,[7] beat[8] Cut's saddle, put a few flocks[9] in
the point.[10] The poor jade[11] is wrung in the withers,[12] out of
all cess.[13]

ENTER CARRIER 2

Carrier 2 Peas and beans[14] are as dank[15] here[16] as a dog,[17] and
that is the next[18] way to give poor jades the bots.[19] This
house[20] is turned upside down since Robin Ostler died.

Carrier 1 Poor fellow never joyed[21] since the price of oats rose, it
was the death of him.

Carrier 2 I think this be the most villainous house in all London
road[22] for fleas. I am stung like a tench.[23]

Carrier 1 Like a tench! By the masse there is ne'er a king in

4 loaded
5 stableman, groom
6 straightaway, immediately
7 the ostler
8 soften/shape by beating
9 tufts of wool
10 pommel (protuberant front part of a saddle)
11 worn-out draught horse
12 wrung in the withers = being squeezed/pressed on the high part of the
back, between the shoulder blades
13 out of all cess = constantly
14 food for animals as well as for men
15 watery
16 at this inn
17 a derisive negative of no precise meaning
18 shortest, most direct
19 maggots
20 inn
21 was happy
22 London road = the road to London
23 like a tench = so that I look like a red-spotted fish

Christendom[24] could be better bit than I have been since the first cock.[25]

Carrier 2 Why, they will allow us ne'er a jordan,[26] and then we leak[27] in your chimney,[28] and your chamber-lye[29] breeds fleas like a loach.[30]

Carrier 1 What, Ostler! Come away[31] and be hanged, come away!

Carrier 2 I have a gammon[32] of bacon, and two razes[33] of ginger, to be delivered as far as Charing Cross.[34]

Carrier 1 God's body, the turkeys in my pannier are quite starved. What, Ostler? A plague on thee, hast thou never an eye in thy head? Canst not hear? And[35] t'were not as good deed as drink,[36] to break the pate[37] on thee, I am[38] a very villain. Come and be hanged! Hast no faith in thee?

The modern reader or listener can, I am convinced, truly tell the one unnamed character from the other, so beautifully evocative is their speech. But without full explanation of words that

24 Folio; Quarto: king christen
25 cock-crow
26 chamber pot
27 urinate
28 your chimney = the fireplace
29 chamber-lye = urine
30 quick-breeding fish
31 come away = get on with it, come on out here
32 ham, haunch
33 roots
34 on the far side of London
35 and if
36 good deed as drink = good a deed as drinking (which of course is very good indeed)
37 break the pate on thee = crack open your head
38 may be called

have over the years shifted in meaning, and usages that have been altered, neither the modern reader nor the modern listener is likely to be equipped for anything like full comprehension.

I believe annotations of this sort create the necessary bridges, from Shakespeare's four-centuries-old English across to ours. Some readers, to be sure, will be able to comprehend unusual, historically different meanings without any glosses. Those not familiar with the modern meaning of particular words will easily find clear, simple definitions in any modern dictionary. But most readers are not likely to understand Shakespeare's intended meaning, absent such glosses as I here offer.

I have followed the "unexpurgated" 1598 *Quarto* text rather than the "sanitized" (expletives-deleted) 1623 *Folio*. Variations from the *Quarto* are recorded in the Notes.

My annotation practices have followed the same principles used in *The Annotated Milton,* published in 1999, and in my annotated editions of *Hamlet,* published (as the initial volume in this series) in 2003, *Romeo and Juliet* (2004), *Macbeth* (2004), *Othello* (2005), and *The Taming of the Shrew* (2005). Classroom experience has validated these editions. Classes of mixed upper-level undergraduates and graduate students have more quickly and thoroughly transcended language barriers than ever before. This allows the teacher, or a general reader without a teacher, to move more promptly and confidently to the nonlinguistic matters that have made Shakespeare and Milton great and important poets.

It is the inevitable forces of linguistic change, operant in all living tongues, which have inevitably created such wide degrees of obstacles to ready comprehension—not only sharply different meanings, but subtle, partial shifts in meaning that allow us to think we understand when, alas, we do not. Speakers of related languages like Dutch and German also experience this shifting of the linguistic ground. Like early Modern English (ca. 1600) and the Modern English now current, those languages are too close for those who know only one language, and not the other, to be readily able always to recognize what they correctly understand and what they do not. When, for example, a speaker of Dutch says, "Men kofer is kapot," a speaker of German will know that something belonging to the Dutchman is broken ("kapot" = "kaputt" in German, and "men" = "mein"). But without more linguistic awareness than the average person is apt to have, the German speaker will not identify "kofer" ("trunk" in Dutch) with "Körper"—a modern German word meaning "physique, build, body." The closest word to "kofer" in modern German, indeed, is "Scrankkoffer," which is too large a leap for ready comprehension. Speakers of different Romance languages (French, Spanish, Italian), and all other related but not identical tongues, all experience these difficulties, as well as the difficulty of understanding a text written in their own language five, or six, or seven hundred years earlier. Shakespeare's English is not yet so old that it requires, like many historical texts in French and German, or like Old English texts—for example, *Beowulf*—a modern translation. Much poetry evaporates in translation: language is immensely particular. The sheer *sound* of Dante in thirteenth-century Italian is profoundly worth preserving. So too is the sound of Shakespeare.

Readers should have no problem with the silent "e." Except in the few instances where modern usage syllabifies the "e," whenever an "e" in Shakespeare is *not* silent, it is marked "è." The notation used for prosody, which is also used in the explanation of Elizabethan pronunciation, follows the extremely simple form of my *From Stress to Stress: An Autobiography of English Prosody* (see

"Further Reading," near the end of this book). Syllables with metrical stress are capitalized; all other syllables are in lower case letters. I have managed to employ normalized Elizabethan spellings, in most indications of pronunciation, but I have sometimes been obliged to deviate, in the higher interest of being understood.

I have annotated, as well, a limited number of such other matters, sometimes of interpretation, sometimes of general or historical relevance, as have seemed to me seriously worthy of inclusion. These annotations have been most carefully restricted: this is not intended to be a book of literary commentary. It is for that reason that the glossing of metaphors has been severely restricted. There is almost literally no end to discussion and/or analysis of metaphor, especially in Shakespeare. To yield to temptation might well be to double or triple the size of this book—and would also change it from a historically oriented language guide to a work of an unsteadily mixed nature. In the process, I believe, neither language nor literature would be well or clearly served.

Where it seemed useful, and not obstructive of important textual matters, I have modernized spelling, including capitalization. Spelling is not on the whole a basic issue, but punctuation and lineation must be given high respect. The Quarto and the Folio use few exclamation marks or semicolons, which is to be sure a matter of the conventions of a very different era. Still, our modern preferences cannot be lightly substituted for what is, after a fashion, the closest thing to a Shakespeare manuscript we are likely ever to have. We do not know whether these particular seventeenth-century printers, like most of that time, were responsible for question marks, commas, periods and, especially, all-purpose colons, or whether these particular printers tried to follow their handwritten sources. Nor do we know if those sources, or what part thereof, might have been in Shakespeare's own hand. But in spite of these equivocations and uncertainties, it remains true that, to a very considerable extent, punctuation tends to result from just how the mind responsible for that punctuating *hears* the text. And twenty-first-century minds have no business, in such matters, overruling seventeenth-century ones. Whoever the compositors were, they were more or less Shakespeare's contemporaries, and we are not.

Accordingly, when the original printed text uses a comma, we are being signaled that *they* (whoever "they" were) heard the text, not coming to a syntactic stop, but continuing to some later stopping point. To replace commas with editorial periods is thus risky and on the whole an undesirable practice. (The dramatic action of a tragedy, to be sure, may require us, for twenty-first-century readers, to highlight what four-hundred-year-old punctuation standards may not make clear—and may even, at times, misrepresent.)

When the printed text has a colon, what we are being signaled is that *they* heard a syntactic stop—though not necessarily or even usually the particular kind of syntactic stop we associate, today, with the colon. It is therefore inappropriate to substitute editorial commas for original colons. It is also inappropriate to employ editorial colons when *their* syntactic usage of colons does not match ours. In general, the closest thing to *their* syntactic sense of the colon is our (and their) period.

The printed interrogation (question) marks, too, merit extremely respectful handling, in a play like *Henry the Fourth, Part One*. In particular, editorial exclamation marks should very rarely be substituted for interrogation marks.

It follows from these considerations that the movement and sometimes the meaning of what we must take to be Shakespeare's *play* will at times be different, depending on whose punctuation we follow, *theirs* or our own. I have tried, here, to use the printed seventeenth-century text as a guide to both *hearing* and *understanding* what Shakespeare wrote.

Since the original printed texts of (there not being, as there never are for Shakespeare, any surviving manuscripts) are frequently careless as well as self-contradictory, I have been relatively free with the wording of stage directions—and in some cases have added brief directions, to indicate who is speaking to whom. I have made no emendations; I have necessarily been obliged to make choices. Textual decisions have been annotated when the differences between or among the original printed texts seem either marked or of unusual interest.

In the interests of compactness and brevity, I have employed in my annotations (as consistently as I am able) a number of stylistic and typographical devices:

- The annotation of a single word does not repeat that word

- The annotation of more than one word repeats the words being annotated, which are followed by an equals sign and then by the annotation; the footnote number in the text is placed after the last of the words being annotated

- In annotations of a single word, alternative meanings are usually separated by commas; if there are distinctly different ranges of meaning, the annotations are separated by arabic numerals inside parentheses—(1), (2), and so on; in more complexly worded annotations, alternative meanings expressed by a single word are linked by a forward slash, or solidus: /

- Explanations of textual meaning are not in parentheses; comments about textual meaning are

- Except for proper nouns, the word at the beginning of all annotations is in lower case

- Uncertainties are followed by a question mark, set in parentheses: (?)

- When particularly relevant, "translations" into twenty-first-century English have been added, in parentheses

- Annotations of repeated words are *not* repeated. Explanations of the *first* instance of such common words are followed by the sign ⋆. Readers may easily track down the first annotation, using the brief Finding List at the back of the book. Words with entirely separate meanings are annotated *only* for meanings no longer current in Modern English.

The most important typographical device here employed is the sign ⋆ placed after the first (and only) annotation of words and phrases occurring more than once. There is an alphabetically arranged listing of such words and phrases in the Finding List at the back of the book. The Finding List contains no annotations but simply gives the words or phrases themselves and the numbers of the relevant act, the scene within that act, and the footnote number within that scene for the word's first occurrence.

INTRODUCTION

T his is the first of the "history" plays to appear in *The Annotated Shakespeare* series. Three basic matters must therefore be briefly dealt with, before *Henry IV, Part One* can be considered:

First, what is the actual historical record?

Second, what seems to have been the attitude to that record, in Elizabethan England?

Third, what in general is Shakespeare's approach to that record?

The Historical Record

Standard histories of England are in agreement: "It was Richard," King of England from 1377 to 1399, and the immediate predecessor of Henry IV, "who made civil war inevitable."[1] Richard II was in many respects a perfectly normal late medieval ruler, absolutist, enormously fond of splendor and magnificent shows of all sorts. The son of the famous "Black Prince," he had inherited the crown at age ten; in his early years on the throne, he was guided and directed by John of Gaunt, Duke of Lancaster (Henry IV's father). Richard was egocentric and enormously confident; he was also immensely extravagant; but, again, his behavior is largely in the best of royal traditions.

Lacking a controlling hand on either his ego or his spending, he overspent hugely, and then attempted to recoup by oppression and confiscation. Things went from bad to worse. The details cannot be set out, here; it was the most dangerous of his seizures, that of the great estates of John of Gaunt, who died in 1399, which ultimately undid him. Richard had previously sent Henry Bolingbroke, Gaunt's oldest son, into exile. Confiscation of his vast estates, and Richard's badly timed military expedition to Ireland, brought Bolingbroke back to England. After much maneuvering, and some fighting, he deposed (and later murdered) Richard and, though he clearly did not have the strongest claim to the throne, succeeded in having himself proclaimed king. (Shakespeare deals with these events in *Richard II*.) To appease critics of his strong-armed behavior, Henry pledged himself to go to the Holy Land, on a Crusade. Circumstances at home never permitted that to happen. He ruled until his death in 1413.

This is the bare historical backdrop to Henry's opening speech, "shaken [and] . . . wan with care."

Elizabethan Attitudes to the Historical Record

Documentation of Elizabethan attitudes is, in general, a piecemeal, flawed affair. For easily understandable reasons, this is particularly true of attitudes toward royalty and governmental processes.[2] Most of the documents that survive are, for equally understandable reasons, written by and expressive of the views and feelings of the relatively small lettered classes. (It is estimated that some 90 percent of the population, in Shakespeare's time, could neither read nor write.) To be sure, there is plain evidence, as early as 1381, of contrarian feelings and events. Early in Richard II's reign, for example, there was a large-scale peasant rebellion, during which as many as a hundred thousand dissidents marched on, took, and did considerable damage to London, especially to wealthy households (burned) and householders (murdered). But there is no reason to believe that contrarian attitudes of any sort represented the approaches that overwhelmingly prevailed in Elizabethan England.

It is difficult for twenty-first-century minds to realize how completely basic, and vitally important, were the monarchy and the social order that existed under its aegis. What made civilized life possible, it was generally realized, was order. This is less a philosophic principle than a clear understanding that disorder produced a nonfunctional society. "Rational" is still a highly positive adjective, but in Shakespeare's England it was much more than that. "The conception of order is so taken for granted, so much part of the collective mind of the people, that it is hardly mentioned except in explicitly didactic passages."[3] "A country owes everything to a good prince," wrote Erasmus earlier in the sixteenth century. The prince must "be a good man for the common good," he goes on, "or a bad one, bringing general destruction."[4] It was clear to most of Shakespeare's countrymen that "general destruction" was indeed precisely what a bad ruler brought. The track record of bad English monarchs was arguably no worse than that of bad monarchs everywhere, but it remained frighteningly bad. The bloody, futile Wars of the Roses, in the latter part of the fifteenth century, did not directly concern the populace; the prolonged, savage fighting was all about succession to the throne and aristocratic entitlement. But the spoilage and carnage were worth remembering and, in fact, were long remembered. Elizabethan England remained, however, brawlingly, fundamentally optimistic. "Man was the measure of all things, for God had created man in his own image, and endowed him with the power of reason whereby to understand the divine order of creation. . . . They did not expect the laws of reason to fail them anywhere: divine order was universal. And if it seemed, sometimes, to be abrogated, this was due to human incompetence, not to divine negligence. . . . This confidence that inspired the courage of the discoverers ['explorers'] also inspired the artists."[5]

Perhaps the most objective standard we have, in judging Elizabethan attitudes to history, is William Harrison's *Description of England* (1687). This large, clearly written compendium deals, so far as possible, with the country's physical and social characteristics. Government, topography, people, dogs, food, quarrying—Harrison touches on everything, and from one proud perspective only. He proposes to celebrate, and in the "vulgar" tongue of his people, the glories that England had come to possess. The editor of a 1968 edition, Georges Edelen, frames this celebratory work against the vast, relatively recent changes England had experienced:"Public change is of course a constant of human existence, but the rate of change is not. In some ages transitions . . . are so slow, even, and predictable as to be almost imperceptibly absorbed by those affected. The other times the gradient becomes much steeper; not only specific developments but the dominance of change forces itself upon the consciousness. *With this heightened realization of transience comes the impulse to describe, to come to terms with the novel by verbal ordering, to weigh [things] against the past.*"[6]

This process seems to me to represent the fundamental historical concerns of both Shakespeare's countrymen and Shakespeare himself. Consider the great capital city, London: "In 1500, ten

European cities, excluding Constantinople, had more inhabitants than London and six others had roughly the same population; in 1600, only two European urban places—Naples and Paris—exceeded the English capital in size, and neither by a very large margin. . . . To look at this growth from a domestic perspective, in 1500 London was four times larger than the next most populous cities in England and Wales, more than fifteen times larger in 1600, and perhaps twenty times larger in 1700."[7] And in London, "as the half century turned, the pressures and consequences of . . . novel economic and spiritual uncertainties began to work their changes. . . . [Men] had come to live with a newly insecure throne, a disturbingly imprecise God and, worst of all, severely fluctuating profits in a world whose boundaries (in every sense) were falling away into the dimly perceived distance. . . . The turbulent years of the mid-sixteenth century saw London's commercial community embarking upon an unprecedented series of novel and highly speculative ventures."[8] At a time of unusual and unusually rapid social and economic change, accompanied by the pressure of varying and often threatening international involvements, Elizabethans quite naturally felt a strong need to know where they had come from and where they thought they had come to.

History as art and entertainment is what Shakespeare offered them—and as Suzanne Langer beautifully and persuasively argues, "The primary function of art is to objectify feeling so that we can contemplate and understand it. . . . Irwin Edman remarks . . . that our emotions are largely Shakespeare's poetry."[9]

Shakespeare's Approach to History

When John Milton (born in 1607) wanted to research historical issues, he consulted his private library as well as the libraries of prosperous and scholarly minded friends. As a university graduate, and son of a wealthy man of legal affairs, Milton moved easily in cultivated, literate society. He had originally intended to become a clergyman, then the most learned of learned professions. He was well trained in Latin, Greek, Hebrew, French, and Italian, and knew at least some Spanish and Old English (Anglo-Saxon). He had made the Grand Tour of Europe, everywhere he went conversing with the most highly educated of men.

Shakespeare was the son of an ambitious but ultimately unsuccessful rural merchant. From what we know of his earlier years, before he emerged as a meteoric success in London's commercial theater, Shakespeare may or may not have spent some time in the houses of more prosperous folk (just as he may or may not have been a Catholic), but certainly not in search of relatively arcane knowledge or, even less likely, as the confidant of people who had first- or second-hand knowledge of English history. We have no idea whatever to whom, once in London, he might possibly have spoken, about such matters; the answer may well be "No one."

For we do have reasonably clear ideas of the printed sources Shakespeare could and almost certainly did make use of, in acquiring the fundamental historical information he required for plays like *Henry the Fourth, Part One.* His primary source was Raphael Holinshed's *Chronicles of England,* in the second edition (1587). What in Holinshed he altered, or simply passed over, shapes a useful guide to his historical approach. The characters of Sir Walter Blunt, Mortimer, and Sir Richard Vernon are almost entirely of Shakespeare's invention: all are little more than names, in Holinshed. Glendower is both vastly amplified and wonderfully refined: to Holinshed he was little more than a Welsh barbarian of magical proclivities and great savagery. Hotspur is an accomplished military leader, in Holinshed, but otherwise essentially bland; his pert wife is entirely Shakespeare's creation, as are his impatient nature, his sometimes rough but always effective wit, and his confrontations with Glendower. The rebels' elaborate pre-battle "contract" is noted in Holinshed, but without any detail. Lord John of Lancaster, in fact aged only thirteen at the time, is essentially Shakespeare's invention.

The affecting, tortured relationship between the King and his son, profoundly central to the play, is also Shakespeare's invention. And the immense deepening of this relationship, by means of the powerful sub-plots and graphic details of Hal's interaction with Falstaff and his crew of criminals, has so far as we know no historical source. Shakespeare did not invent the play's large and vital shift in the actual ages of the King, Hal, and Hotspur, all once again dramatically central. The King was thirty-seven at the Shrewsbury battle, Hotspur was thirty-nine, and Hal was only sixteen. Significantly, Shakespeare probably borrowed these adjustments in chronology from book 3 of Samuel Daniel's *The First Four Books of the Civil Wars* . . . (1595). Daniel was a very good poet (and an accomplished sonneteer), with a deft writerly sense. Here is his fine conjuring up of the direct meeting in battle of Hotspur and Hal, a passage Daniel addressed to the King:

> There shall young Hotspur with a fury lead
> Meet with thy forward son, as fierce as he.
> There warlike Worcester long experiencèd
> In foreign arms shall come t'encounter thee.
> There Douglas to thy Stafford shall make head,
> There Vernon for thy valiant Blunt shall be,
> There shalt thou find a doubtful, bloody day,
> Though sickness keep Northumberland away.
>
> (book 3, stanza 97)

We can respond to this poetry; Shakespeare surely did, and seems to have come away with useful perspectives.

There are a few other possible sources, much debated upon but not necessary to be considered here. What can be safely concluded from this brief overview is that Shakespeare, like his contemporaries, probably neither more nor less, was indeed interested in the history of England, but was even more interested in creating an effective dramatic vehicle. He does not, strictly speaking, betray history. But neither does he allow it to stand in the way of his overriding concerns as a shiningly successful commercial playwright. He ought not to be consulted as an historical authority, in this or in any of his history plays. How much he valued history per se we have no absolutely no notion. But we know how hungrily he devoured good stories, invariably turning them into still better theater.

The Play

Henry the Fourth, Part One, is usually dated 1598, when its publication was officially registered, though it was probably written in 1596–97 and first performed in 1597. By no means the longest of Shakespeare's plays, its organization ("structure") and presentation ("style") are so taut and so deftly, complexly interwoven that the dramatic effect is at all points both complete and continuously, miraculously in balance. The play's movement ("pace") is not at all uniform. But nothing grave, like the King's somber, self-tortured opening speech, seems to progress in any way slowly:

> So shaken as we are, so wan with care,
> Find we a time for frightèd peace to pant,
> And breathe short-winded accents of new broils

To be commenced in stronds afar remote.
No more the thirsty entrance of this soil
Shall daub her lips with her own children's blood.

(1.1.1–6)

The King is not alone, but in many ways he might as well be. He is setting out his feelings and hopes, his agenda for the future and justification for the recent past, quite as much for himself as for the assembled members of his royal court. We begin to suspect that he desperately wants to believe what he is saying aloud, to his ministers. But he does not, we also suspect, either believe or feel that they believe. Perhaps, indeed, he does not know what to believe, or whom.

The second scene of the first act, in prose rather verse, is nowhere near so freighted with emotional brews. Hal is breezily, casually cutting to his fat friend, Falstaff, and the quick-scurrying words fairly blow across either the page or the stage:

Falstaff Now Hal, what time of day is it, lad?

Hal Thou art so fat-witted with drinking of old sack, and unbuttoning thee after supper, and sleeping upon benches after noon, that thou hast forgotten to demand that truly which thou wouldst truly know. What a divel hast thou to do with the time of the day? Unless hours were cups of sack, and minutes capons, and clocks the tongues of bawds, and dials the signs of leaping-houses, and the blessèd sun himself a fair hot wench in flame-colored taffeta, I see no reason why thou shouldst be so superfluous, to demand the time of the day.

(1.2.1–11)

Barroom prattle has never been more accurately evoked. And yet, this is plainly no mere chatter. Hal jokes, but somehow seriously, just as Falstaff assumes an avuncular tone with his royal pal, but never dares carry it too far. The dialogue between these two takes us very far from the King's palace, but yet not so very far at all. And by the end of this scene, when Falstaff and the others have left and Hal is alone, we see precisely how the two nominally different settings are irremediably joined. Hal's monologue, distinctly anticipating those of Hamlet (as yet unwritten), switches into the verse of the first scene. But how different the poetry is, and how different the son is from the father!

Hal I know you all, and will a while uphold
    The unyoked humor of your idleness.
    Yet herein will I imitate the sun,
    Who doth permit the base contagious clouds
    To smother up his beauty from the world,
    That when he please again to be himself,
    Being wanted, he may be more wondered at
    By breaking through the foul and ugly mists
    Of vapors, that did seem to strangle him.
    If all the year were playing holidays,
    To sport would be as tedious as to work.
    But when they seldom come, they wished-for come,
    And nothing pleaseth but rare accidents.
    So when this loose behavior I throw off,
    And pay the debt I never promised,
    By how much better than my word I am,
    By so much shall I falsify men's hopes . . .

                        (1.2.176–90)

This both is and is not the Hal we have been watching. The entire play has to be unrolled for us, before we fully understand, before we see how the intricately chiseled elements of the narrative fit into their final, operative state. But in another way, inchoate but also sensate, we already know. This being Shakespeare at his best, events may come at us freshly, unanticipated. But they are also more than fully predicated on, and thus in a way predicted by, what has come before.

Falstaff, one of the greatest comedic characters in all of world literature, is like Don Quijote not totally comic—and as Hamlet, too, is not totally tragic, and often very comic indeed. Queen Elizabeth was so fascinated by the character that, as royalty will, she let it be known that more of him was wanted. *The Merry Wives of Windsor,* featuring Falstaff, was written and performed before the end of 1597. It is not one of Shakespeare's greatest works, though Giuseppe Verdi wrote one of his greatest operas, called simply *Falstaff,* around the contortions of its plot. But in *Henry the Fourth, Part One,* Falstaff is unmatched:

Falstaff   I am accursed to rob in that thief's company. The rascal
       hath removed my horse, and tied him I know not where. If I
       travel but four foot by the squier further afoot, I shall break
       my wind. Well, I doubt not but to die a fair death for all this, if
       I scape hanging for killing that rogue. I have forsworn his
       company hourly any time this two and twenty years, and yet I
       am bewitched with the rogue's company. If the rascal have
       not given me medicines to make me love him, I'll be hanged.
       It could not be else, I have drunk medicines. Poins, Hal, a
       plague upon you both! Bardolph, Peto, I'll starve ere I'll rob a
       foot further! And 'twere not as good a deed as drink to turn

true man, and to leave these rogues, I am the veriest varlet that ever chewed with a tooth. Eight yards of uneven ground is threescore and ten miles afoot with me, and the stony-hearted villains know it well enough. A plague upon it when thieves cannot be true one to another!

(2.2.9–24)

One could build an entire theory of comedy on a monologue like this. Anyone who has ever acted on a stage will fairly drool at the prospect of performing Falstaff.

Hotspur cannot be neglected, though in a brief introductory essay he cannot be done full justice.

Worcester   You start away,
And lend no ear unto my purposes.
Those prisoners you shall keep.
Hotspur   Nay, I will. That's flat.
He said he would not ransom *Mortimer,*
Forbade my tongue to speak of *Mortimer,*
But I will find him when he lies asleep,
And in his eare I'll holla *Mortimer,*
Nay, I'll have a starling shall be taught to speak
Nothing but *Mortimer,* and give it him
To keep his anger still in motion.
Worcester Hear you cousin. A word.
Hotspu   All studies here I solemnly defy,
Save how to gall and pinch this Bolingbroke,
And that same sword-and-buckler Prince of Wales.
But that I think his father loves him not,
And would be glad he met with some mischance,
I would have him poisoned with a pot of ale.

Worcester Farewell kinsman, I'll talk to you
   When you are better tempered to attend.

(1.3.215–34)

This is so out of control that it amounts to comedy. And at the same time, not only is it profoundly serious, but by the final scenes of the play we fully understand how this is precisely the flaw that brings Hotspur down.

The poet Mark Van Doren, writing more than sixty-five years ago, wrapped all of this, and more, in a very few words: "No play of Shakespeare's is better than 'Henry IV.' Certain subsequent ones may show him more settled in the maturity which he here attains at a single bound, but nothing that he wrote is more crowded with life. . . . The poetry of Hotspur and the prose of Falstaff have never been surpassed in their respective categories; the History as a dramatic form ripens here to a point past which no further growth is possible."[10]

Notes

1. Keith Feiling, *A History of England* (New York: McGraw-Hill, 1948), 264.

2. In 1599, John Hayward published *The First Part of the Life and Reign of King Henry IV,* dedicating it to the Earl of Essex. Because Queen Elizabeth worried that the book's account of the deposition of Richard II was suggestive of what might (or ought to) happen to her, Hayward was brought before the Star Chamber, accused of treason, and imprisoned.

3. E. M. W. Tillyard, *The Elizabethan World Picture* (London: Chatto and Windus, 1943), 18.

4. Desiderius Erasmus, *The Education of a Christian Prince,* trans. Lester K. Born (New York: Octagon Books, 1987), 141, 156.

5. John Buxton, *Elizabethan Taste* (Atlantic Highlands, N.J.: Humanities Press, 1963), 33–35.

6. William Harrison, *The Description of England: The Classic Contemporary [1577] Account of Tudor Social Life,* ed. Georges Edelen (Washington, D.C.: Folger

Shakespeare Library, 1968; repr., New York: Dover, 1994), xxix (emphasis added).

7. David Harris Sacks, "London's Dominion: The Metropolis, the Market Economy, and the State," in *Material London, ca. 1600,* ed. Lena Cowen Orlin (Philadelphia: University of Pennsylvania Press, 2000), 22.

8. James McDermott, *Martin Frobisher: Elizabethan Privateer* (New Haven and London: Yale University Press, 2001) 21, 26.

9. Susanne Langer, "The Cultural Importance of Art," in Langer, *Philosophical Sketches* (Baltimore: Johns Hopkins University Press, 1962), 90, 93.

10. Mark Van Doren, *Shakespeare* (New York: Holt, 1939), 97.

SOME ESSENTIALS OF THE
SHAKESPEAREAN STAGE

The Stage

- There was no *scenery* (backdrops, flats, and so on).

- Compared to today's elaborate, high-tech productions, the Elizabethan stage had few *on-stage* props. These were mostly handheld: a sword or dagger, a torch or candle, a cup or flask. Larger props, such as furniture, were used sparingly.

- Costumes (some of which were upper-class castoffs, belonging to the individual actors) were elaborate. As in most premodern and very hierarchical societies, clothing was the distinctive mark of who and what a person was.

- What the actors *spoke,* accordingly, contained both the dramatic and narrative material we have come to expect in a theater (or movie house) and (1) the setting, including details of the time of day, the weather, and so on, and (2) the occasion. The *dramaturgy* is thus very different from that of our own time, requiring much more attention to verbal and gestural matters. Strict realism was neither intended nor, under the circumstances, possible.

- There was *no curtain*. Actors entered and left via doors in the back of the stage, behind which was the "tiring-room," where actors put on or changed their costumes.

- In *public theaters* (which were open-air structures), there was no *lighting;* performances could take place only in daylight hours.

- For *private* theaters, located in large halls of aristocratic houses, candlelight illumination was possible.

The Actors

- Actors worked in *professional,* for-profit companies, sometimes organized and owned by other actors, and sometimes by entrepreneurs who could afford to erect or rent the company's building. Public theaters could hold, on average, two thousand playgoers, most of whom viewed and listened while standing. Significant profits could be and were made. Private theaters were smaller, more exclusive.

- There was *no director.* A book-holder/prompter/props manager, standing in the tiring-room behind the backstage doors, worked from a text marked with entrances and exits and notations of any special effects required for that particular script. A few such books have survived. Actors had texts only of their own parts, speeches being cued to a few prior words. There were few and often no rehearsals, in our modern use of the term, though there was often some coaching of individuals. Since Shakespeare's England was largely an oral culture, actors learned their parts rapidly and retained them for years. This was *repertory* theater, repeating popular plays and introducing some new ones each season.

- *Women* were not permitted on the professional stage. Most female roles were acted by boys; elderly women were played by grown men.

The Audience

- London's professional theater operated in what might be called a "red-light" district, featuring brothels, restaurants, and the kind of *open-air entertainment* then most popular, like bear-baiting (in which a bear, tied to a stake, was set on by dogs).

- A theater audience, like most of the population of Shakespeare's England, was largely made up of *illiterates*. Being able to read and write, however, had nothing to do with intelligence or concern with language, narrative, and characterization. People attracted to the theater tended to be both extremely verbal and extremely volatile. Actors were sometimes attacked, when the audience was dissatisfied; quarrels and fights were relatively common. Women were regularly in attendance, though no reliable statistics exist.

- Drama did not have the cultural esteem it has in our time, and plays were not regularly printed. Shakespeare's often appeared in book form, but not with any supervision or other involvement on his part. He wrote a good deal of nondramatic poetry as well, yet so far as we know he did not authorize or supervise *any* work of his that appeared in print during his lifetime.

- Playgoers, who had paid good money to see and hear, plainly gave dramatic performances careful, detailed attention. For some closer examination of such matters, see Burton Raffel, "Who Heard the Rhymes and How: Shakespeare's Dramaturgical Signals," *Oral Tradition* 11 (October 1996): 190–221, and Raffel, "Metrical Dramaturgy in Shakespeare's Earlier Plays," *CEA Critic* 57 (Spring–Summer 1995): 51–65.

Henry the Fourth, Part One

CHARACTERS (DRAMATIS PERSONAE)

Henry IV (King of England)

Hal (Henry, Prince of Wales, the King's older son)

John (Lord of Lancaster, the King's younger son)

Earl of Westmoreland

Sir Walter Blunt

Thomas Percy (Earl of Worcester[1])

Henry Percy (his brother, Earl of Northumberland)

Hotspur (Henry Percy the younger, Northumberland's son)

Lady Percy (Hotspur's wife, Mortimer's sister)

Edmund Mortimer (Earl of March)

Lady Mortimer (Mortimer's wife, Glendower's daughter)

Owen Glendower

Douglas

Sir Richard Vernon

Richard Scroop (Archbishop of York)

Sir Michael (friend of the Archbishop of York)

Sir John Falstaff

Poins, Peto, Bardolph, Gadshill (Falstaff's companions)

Mistress Quickly (hostess[2] of The Boar's Head, an inn in
    Eastcheap)

*Sheriff, Vintner, Chamberlain,[3] Two Carriers,[4] Ostler,[5] Messengers,
    Travelers, Attendants*

1 WUster
2 mistress, person in charge★
3 waiter/servant at an inn★
4 teamsters★
5 stableman, groom★

Act I

SCENE I
London, the palace

ENTER THE KING, JOHN, WESTMORELAND,
SIR WALTER BLUNT, WITH OTHERS

King So[1] shaken as we[2] are, so wan with care,
    Find[3] we a time for frighted peace to pant,
    And breathe short-winded[4] accents of new broils[5]
    To be commenced in stronds[6] afar remote.
    No more the thirsty entrance[7] of this soil   5
    Shall daub[8] her lips with her own children's blood,

1 as
2 the royal "we," meaning "I"
3 obtain, come to have, experience
4 short-winded = hard to breathe
5 accents of new broils = sounds/tones/words of fresh tumult/quarrels★ (and
   BREATHE short WINded ACcents OF new BROILS)
6 shores ("strands")
7 opening, mouth (metaphoric)
8 coat, cover, smear, soil

3

No more shall trenching[9] war channel[10] her[11] fields,
Nor bruise[12] her flowrets[13] with the armèd hoofs
Of hostile paces.[14] Those opposèd[15] eyes,
Which like the meteors of a troubled[16] heaven,
All[17] of one nature, of[18] one substance[19] bred,
Did lately meet in the intestine shock[20]
And furious close[21] of civil[22] butchery,
Shall now in mutual well-beseeming[23] ranks
March all one way, and be no more[24] opposed
Against acquaintance, kindred, and allies.
The edge[25] of war, like an ill[26]-sheathèd knife,[27]
No more shall cut his[28] master. Therefore friends,
As far as to the sepulcher[29] of Christ,

10

15

---

9 (1) encroaching, infringing, (2) cutting, furrowing, (3) the digging of ditches/trenches, in siege warfare, (4) the digging of defensive trenches around a site
10 groove, furrow (verb)
11 England ("the soil")
12 crush, mangle
13 small flowers (flower-ettes)
14 steps, walking or running
15 hostile ("in opposition/conflict")
16 agitated, disordered
17 are all
18 all of
19 material (metaphoric)
20 intestine shock = domestic/internal collision/encounter/clashing
21 grappling, struggles
22 communal ("confined to the members of one community")*
23 mutual well-beseeming = reciprocal/friendly/united and deep-seated appropriateness
24 longer
25 blade ("cutting edge")
26 badly
27 the EDGE of WAR like AN ill-SHEAthed KNIFE
28 its
29 burial place (Jerusalem)

Whose soldier now,[30] under whose blessèd cross   20
We are impressèd[31] and engaged[32] to fight,
Forthwith[33] a power[34] of English shall we levy,[35]
Whose arms were molded[36] in their mothers' womb
To chase[37] these pagans in those holy fields,
Over whose acres walked those blessèd feet   25
Which fourteen hundred years ago were nailed
For our advantage[38] on the bitter cross.
But this our purpose[39] now is twelve month old,
And bootless[40] 'tis to tell you we will go.[41]
Therefore we meet not[42] now. Then let me hear   30
Of[43] you, my gentle[44] cousin[45] Westmoreland,[46]
What yesternight[47] our council did decree
In forwarding[48] this dear expedience.[49]

---

30 now we have become/are
31 levied, conscripted (to serve militarily)
32 obliged
33 without delay, immediately
34 army★
35 raise, conscript
36 produced, shaped
37 to chase = in order to hunt/pursue
38 profit, gain★
39 intention★
40 useless★
41 (he does not ever go)
42 therefore we meet not = this is not why we are meeting
43 from
44 noble, well-bred★
45 used for virtually all family members, regardless of closeness of relationship
46 titled men are known either by their family name or by their title without any name attached
47 last night
48 advancing, promoting
49 dear expedience = cherished expedition/enterprise

Westmoreland My liege.[50] This haste[51] was hot in question,[52]

35   And many limits of the charge[53] set down
       But[54] yesternight. When all athwart[55] there came
       A post[56] from Wales, loaden with heavy news,
       Whose worst was that the noble Mortimer,
       Leading the men of Herefordshire[57] to fight

40   Against the irregular and wild[58] Glendower,
       Was by the rude[59] hands of that Welshman taken,[60]
       A thousand of his people butchered,
       Upon whose dead corpse[61] there was such misuse,[62]
       Such beastly, shameless transformation,[63]

45   By those Welshwomen done, as may not be
       (Without much shame) retold or spoken of.

King   It seems then that the tidings of this broil
       Brake[64] off our business for the Holy Land.

Westmoreland This matched with other[65] did, my gracious lord,

50 feudal/hierarchical superior★
51 urgency
52 hot in question = ardently/violently in dispute/under consideration/
   doubtful and undecided
53 limits of the charge = parameters/boundaries/fixed and precise details of
   the (1) expenses/burdens, (2) tasks/offices/responsibilities, (3) instructions,
   general orders
54 only
55 unexpectedly, at cross-purposes
56 post/express messenger
57 county in W England (HEfirdSHIR)
58 irregular and wild = disorderly/lawless and savage/rebellious/
   uncontrollable
59 barbarous, uncivilized★
60 made captive, captured★
61 (plural)
62 ill usage
63 changing of shape/form (TRANSforMAYseeOWN)
64 broke
65 matched with other = combined/joined★ with other news

For more uneven[66] and unwelcome news   50

Came from the North, and thus it did import.[67]

On Holy Rood[68] day, the gallant[69] Hotspur there,

Young Harry Percy,[70] and brave[71] Archibald,[72]

That ever-valiant and approvèd[73] Scot,

At Holmedon[74] met, where they did spend[75]   55

A sad[76] and bloody hour.

As by discharge[77] of their artillery,

And shape of likelihood,[78] the news was told,[79]

For[80] he that brought them[81] in the very heat[82]

And pride[83] of their contention did take horse,[84]   60

Uncertain of the issue[85] any way.[86]

King Here is a dear, a true industrious[87] friend,

66 irregular
67 convey, communicate, state
68 cross (14 September)
69 (1) daring, brave, (2) courtier-like★
70 Hotspur
71 (1) courageous, (2) fine, splendid, worthy★
72 Douglas
73 experience-tested
74 Humbleton, in Northumberland
75 AT holMAYdun MET where THEY did SPEND
76 (1) grave, serious, (2) sorrowful
77 firing
78 shape of likelihood = of probability
79 reckoned, calculated, evaluated
80 since
81 the news (then considered a plural noun)
82 very heat = true★ rage/passion/excitement
83 highest point
84 take horse = ride off to bring the news
85 result
86 any way = in either direction
87 true industrious = faithful/loyal/genuine★ (1) skillful, clever, (2) zealous, painstaking

Sir Walter Blunt, new lighted[88] from his horse,
Stained with[89] the variation of[90] each soil
65   Betwixt that Holmedon and this seat[91] of ours.
And he hath brought us smooth[92] and welcome news.
The Earl of Douglas is discomfited,[93]
Ten thousand bold Scots, two-and-twenty knights
Balked[94] in their own blood, did Sir Walter see
70   On Holmedon's plains. Of prisoners Hotspur took
Mordake, Earl of Fife, and eldest son
To beaten Douglas, and the Earl of Athol,
Of[95] Murray, Angus, and Menteith.
And is not this an honorable spoil?[96]
A gallant prize? Ha cousin, is it not?

75 *Westmoreland*   In faith[97]
It is a conquest for a prince[98] to boast of.

King   Yea, there thou makst me sad, and makst me sin
In envy, that my Lord Northumberland
Should be the father to so blest a son.

---

88 descended ("alighted")
89 stained with = soiled/dirtied by
90 variation of = changes in
91 governing location ("palace")
92 pleasant, orderly
93 defeated, frustrated
94 heaped, piled
95 syntactically parallel to "of prisoners"
96 honorable spoil = worthy/excellent capture (ONoRAble)
97 Quarto and Folio both confuse, differently, the ascription of "in faith it is"; all editors emend
98 although "prince" does not necessarily refer to a particular person bearing such a title, here the word plainly evokes an unfavorable comparison between gallant, successful Hotspur (who is not a prince) and reckless, dissolute Hal, who is the Prince of Wales

A son who is the theme[99] of honor's tongue,   80
Amongst a grove the very straightest plant,[100]
Who is sweet Fortune's minion[101] and her pride,
Whilst I by looking on the praise of him
See riot[102] and dishonor stain the brow
Of my young Harry.[103] O that it could be proved   85
That some night-tripping[104] fairy had exchanged
In cradle clothes our children where they lay,
And called mine Percy, his Plantagenet.[105]
Then would I have his Harry, and he mine.
But let[106] him from my thoughts. What think you coz[107]   90
Of this young Percy's pride? The prisoners
Which he in this adventure[108] hath surprised[109]
To his own use he keeps, and sends me word
I shall have none but Mordake, Earl of Fife.

Westmoreland This is his uncle's teaching. This is Worcester,[110]   95
Malevolent to you in all aspects,[111]
Which makes him prune himself,[112] and bristle up

99 subject
100 sapling, young tree
101 darling, favorite
102 loose/wanton living, debauchery
103 Hal
104 tripping = light-footed/nimble movement
105 the king's family/dynastic name
106 let him pass/leave
107 familiar form of "cousin"
108 event, venture★
109 seized, captured
110 WUSter
111 asPECTS
112 prune himself = Hotspur preen/plume

The crest[113] of youth against your dignity.[114]

 King   But I have sent for him to answer[115] this.

100 And for this cause a while we must neglect

 Our holy purpose to Jerusalem.

 Cousin, on Wednesday next our council we

 Will hold at Windsor.[116] So inform the lords.

 But come yourself with speed to us again,

105 For more is to be said, and to be done,

 Than out of anger can be uttered.

 Westmoreland I will my liege.

EXEUNT[117]

---

113 feathered tuft on a male bird's head★ (raised in anger or other high
  emotion)
114 nobility, rank, worth, honor★
115 respond to a charge, defend himself
116 Windsor Castle, occupied by British kings since 1066
117 plural of "exit"★

SCENE 2

London, the Prince of Wales' apartments

ENTER THE PRINCE OF WALES AND SIR JOHN FALSTAFF

Falstaff Now Hal, what time of day is it, lad?

Hal   Thou art so fat-witted[1] with drinking of old sack,[2] and
unbuttoning thee after supper, and sleeping upon benches
after noon, that thou hast forgotten to demand[3] that truly[4]
which thou wouldst truly know. What a divel[5] hast thou to   5
do with the time of the day? Unless hours were cups of sack,
and minutes capons,[6] and clocks the tongues of bawds,[7] and
dials the signs of leaping-houses,[8] and the blessèd sun
himself[9] a fair[10] hot wench in flame-colored taffeta,[11] I see
no reason why thou shouldst be so superfluous, to[12] demand   10
the time of the day.

Falstaff Indeed you come near me[13] now Hal, for we that take
purses[14] go by the moon and the seven stars,[15] and not "by

---

1 thick-headed (wit = mind, brain)
2 white wines from Spain and the Canary Islands★
3 ask for★
4 honestly, honorably, correctly★
5 devil (reconstructions of Shakespearean English have a distinct flavor of
modern Irish English)
6 castrated cocks
7 pimps (female or male)
8 brothels
9 virtually no one carried a watch, and the sun had long been used to tell time
10 attractive, beautiful, delightful★
11 silk fabric often worn by prostitutes
12 superfluous, to = immoderate/extravagant as to
13 come near me = touch me closely
14 take purses = seize/steal money pouches (*not* the "bags" carried by women,
now, but small cloth/leather bags with drawstrings, carried by both sexes,
there being no trousers with pockets and no paper money)
15 i.e., at night

Phoebus,[16] he, that wand'ring knight so fair."[17] And I prithee,[18]

15   sweet wag,[19] when thou art king, as[20] God save[21] thy grace[22] –

Majesty I should say, for grace[23] thou wilt have none.

Hal   What, none?

Falstaff No, by my troth,[24] not so much as will serve to be

prologue to an egg and butter.[25]

20 *Hal*   Well, how then? Come, roundly,[26] roundly.

Falstaff Marry[27] then, sweet wag, when thou art king let not us

that are squires[28] of the night's body, be called thieves of the

day's beauty. Let us be Diana's foresters,[29] gentlemen of the

shade, minions of the moon, and let men say we be men of

25   good government,[30] being governed as the sea is, by our

noble and chaste mistress[31] the moon, under whose

countenance[32] we steal.[33]

Hal   Thou sayest well, and it[34] holds well too, for the fortune

16 the sun god
17 probably quoted from a lost ballad
18 prithee = ask, request★
19 young fellow
20 may
21 protect
22 formal mode of address to rulers
23 (1) God's grace/mercy/favor, pardon,★ (2) charm, attractiveness, (3) the grace said by proper people before eating
24 by my troth = by my faith★
25 i.e., meatless food eaten on Fridays, when meat was forbidden, or during Lent: the prologue, or saying of grace, would likely be short, for such meals
26 bluntly, to the point
27 to be sure (exclamation)★
28 attendants to (as squires/pages attended/waited on knights)
29 (1) huntsmen, (2) guardians of forests (important to aristocrats, most of whom hunted)
30 good government = well behaved/controlled/ruled★
31 female form of "master"
32 (1) face, glance, (2) favor, support, patronage
33 (1) rob, (2) sneak about
34 the comparison/metaphor

of us that are the moon's men doth ebb and flow like the sea,
being governed as the sea is by the moon. As for proof, now a   30
purse of gold most resolutely[35] snatched on Monday night
and most dissolutely spent on Tuesday morning, got with
swearing, "Lay by!"[36] and spent with crying, "Bring in!"[37]
now in as low an ebb as the foot of the ladder,[38] and by and
by[39] in as high a flow[40] as the ridge[41] of the gallows.   35

Falstaff By the Lord thou sayst true, lad. And is not my[42] hostess
of the tavern a most sweet wench?

Hal   As the honey of Hibla,[43] my old lad of the castle.[44] And
is not a buff jerkin[45] a most sweet robe of durance?[46]

Falstaff How now?[47] How now, mad wag? What in[48] thy   40
quips[49] and thy quiddities?[50] What a plague[51] have I to do
with a buff jerkin?

35 boldly
36 swearing, "Lay by!" = commanding robbery victims (1) to set down their
   weapons, or (2) to pull over
37 crying, "Bring in!" = calling to a tavern waiter to fetch liquor
38 (1) any ladder, (2) the ladder up which condemned men had to climb, to
   reach the gallows platform
39 soon
40 inward, rising movement of the tide (direct opposite of "ebb")
41 top (from which the gallows rope hangs)
42 not a possessive in the modern sense, but more like "the" or "that"
43 famously fine honey from Sicily
44 "Oldcastle" had been the character's original name; the name had been
   changed by Shakespeare when members of the noble Oldcastle family ob-
   jected
45 buff jerkin = light brown–yellowish leather close-fitting jacket/short coat,
   worn by constables
46 robe of durance = outer garment/clothing that is (1) stout, strong,
   (2) lasting, (3) associated with imprisonment
47 how now? = what?
48 what in = what is this about
49 clever remarks
50 subtleties, sharp arguments
51 what a plague = what the devil

Hal   Why what a pox[52] have I to do with my hostess of the
tavern?

45 *Falstaff* Well, thou hast called her to a reckoning[53] many a time
and oft.

Hal   Did I ever call for thee to pay thy part?[54]

Falstaff No, I'll give thee thy due, thou hast paid all there.

Hal   Yea and elsewhere, so far as my coin[55] would stretch, and
50 where it would not, I have used my credit.

Falstaff Yea, and so used it that were it not here apparent that
thou art heir apparent[56] – But I prithee sweet wag, shall there
be gallows standing in England when thou art king? And
resolution thus fubbed[57] as it is with the rusty curb[58] of old
55 father Antic[59] the law? Do not thou when thou art king hang
a thief.

Hal   No, thou shalt.[60]

Falstaff Shall I? O rare![61] By the Lord I'll be a brave judge.

Hal   Thou judgest false already. I mean thou shalt have[62] the
60 hanging of the thieves, and so become a rare hangman.

Falstaff Well Hal, well. And in some sort[63] it jumps[64] with my

52 loose characterization of various diseases, smallpox, chicken pox, syphilis
53 to a reckoning = for a bill
54 share, division★
55 money (all of which was coin, there being no paper money)
56 heir apparent = next in line to the throne★
57 resolution thus fubbed = determination/steadiness in this way cheated
58 rusty curb = corrupt/foul/surly/antiquated chain/restraint★
59 bizarre, grotesque, ludicrous
60 thou shalt = you will cause the hanging of thieves (including himself)
61 exceptional, excellent, splendid
62 be responsible for
63 way, kind
64 agrees, coincides, suits

humor,[65] as[66] well as waiting in the court,[67] I can tell you.

Hal   For obtaining of suits?[68]

Falstaff Yea, for obtaining of suits, whereof the hangman hath no
   lean[69] wardrobe. 'Sblood,[70] I am as melancholy as a gib[71] cat,   65
   or a lugged[72] bear.

Hal   Or an old lion, or a lover's lute.[73]

Falstaff Yea, or the drone[74] of a Lincolnshire bagpipe.

Hal   What sayest thou to a hare,[75] or the melancholy of
   Moor-ditch?[76]   70

Falstaff Thou hast the most unsavory[77] similes,[78] and art indeed
   the most comparative[79] rascalliest[80] sweet young Prince. But
   Hal, I prithee trouble me no more with vanity. I would to
   God thou and I knew where a commodity[81] of good names
   were to be bought. An old lord of the council rated[82] me the   75

---

65 nature, mood, disposition, character★
66 just as
67 waiting in the court = hanging about (1) the King's court, for favors (2) the
   law court, for the forfeited clothing of condemned men
68 (1) requests for favor, (2) condemned men's clothing
69 slight, thin
70 God's blood (common oath)★
71 castrated
72 baited (chained to a post and tormented by dogs)
73 lover's lute = (?) old and disused?
74 the steady, unchanging bass note
75 "The flesh of hares be hot and dry, ingenderers of melancholy" (William
   Bullein, *Government of Health*, 1558, 90, cited in G. L. Apperson, *The
   Wordsworth Dictionary of Proverbs* [London: Wordsworth, 1993], 185b)
76 London area associated with a singularly foul sewage/drainage canal
77 insipid, unattractive, disagreeable
78 SImiLEEZ (both Quarto and Folio: smiles)
79 comparison-oriented
80 worthless, lower-class
81 convenient supply
82 angrily scolded/reproved

other day in the street about you sir, but I marked him not,[83] and yet he talked very wisely, but I regarded[84] him not, and yet he talked wisely, and in the street too.

Hal   Thou didst well, for wisdom cries out in the streets and
80   no man regards it.[85]

Falstaff O, thou hast damnable[86] iteration, and art indeed able to corrupt a saint. Thou hast done much harm upon[87] me, Hal, God forgive thee for it. Before I knew thee, Hal, I knew nothing, and now am I, if a man should[88] speak truly, little
85   better than one of the wicked. I must give over this life, and I will give it over. By the Lord and[89] I do not, I am a villain.[90] I'll be damned for never a[91] king's son in Christendom.

Hal   Where shall we take a purse tomorrow, Jack?

Falstaff Zounds,[92] where thou wilt, lad, I'll make one.[93] An[94] I
90   do not, call me villain and baffle[95] me.

Hal   I see a good amendment[96] of life in thee, from praying to purse-taking.

---

83 marked him not = paid no attention to him★
84 paid no attention
85 "Wisdom crieth without [outside]; she uttereth her voice in the streets … . and no man regarded" (Prov. 1:20, 24)
86 highly reprehensible / hurtful / pernicious way of repeatedly quoting from scripture
87 Folio: unto
88 must, had to
89 if
90 rascal, scoundrel★
91 never a = no
92 God's wounds★ (OATH)
93 make one = join in
94 if★
95 publicly disgrace
96 reformation, correction★

Falstaff Why Hal, 'tis my vocation,[97] Hal, 'tis no sin for a man to labor in his vocation.

ENTER POINS

Poins! Now shall we know if Gadshill have set a match.[98] O, if men were to be saved by merit, what hole in hell were hot enough for him? This is the most omnipotent[99] villain that ever cried, "Stand!"[100] to a true[101] man.   95

Hal   Good morrow,[102] Ned.

Poins   Good morrow, sweet Hal. What says Monsieur Remorse?[103] What says Sir John sack and sugar?[104] Jack? How agrees[105] the Divel and thee about thy soul, that thou soldest him[106] on Good Friday last, for a cup of Madeira and a cold capon's leg?   100

Hal   Sir John stands to[107] his word, the Devil shall have his bargain, for he[108] was never yet a breaker of proverbs. He will give the Devil his due.   105

Poins   Then art thou[109] damned for keeping thy word with the Devil.

---

97 special divine function
98 have set a match = has arranged a robbery expedition
99 mighty, arrant, unparalleled
100 hands up, stand and deliver, hand it over
101 honest, virtuous
102 morning*
103 scruple, regret, hesitation
104 (?) sugar added to wine
105 bargained
106 to him (the Devil)
107 abides by, will carry out
108 Falstaff
109 Falstaff

110 **Hal**   Else[110] he had[111] been damned for cozening[112] the
Devil.

Poins   But my lads, my lads, tomorrow morning, by four
o'clock early at Gad's Hill,[113] there are pilgrims going to
Canterbury with rich offerings, and traders riding to London
115   with fat purses. I have vizards[114] for you all. You have horses
for yourselves. Gadshill lies[115] tonight in Rochester, I have
bespoke[116] supper tomorrow night in Eastcheap.[117] We may
do it as secure[118] as sleep. If you will go, I will stuff your
purses full of crowns.[119] If you will not, tarry[120] at home and
120   be hanged.

Falstaff   Hear ye, Edward, if I tarry at home and go not, I'll hang
you for going.

Poins   You will, chops?[121]

Falstaff   Hal, wilt thou make one?

125 **Hal**   Who, I rob? I a thief? Not I, by my faith.

Falstaff   There's neither honesty, manhood, nor good fellowship
in thee, nor thou cam'st not of the blood[122] royal, if thou
darest not stand[123] for ten shillings.[124]

110 otherwise★
111 would have
112 cheating, defrauding★
113 (located on the road between London and Rochester)
114 masks
115 sleeps, stays
116 ordered
117 a street in London
118 safely, confidently
119 coins, originally of gold
120 linger, loiter★
121 fat face
122 lineage★
123 act like a friend? commit yourself?
124 the "royal" was an English gold coin, worth 10 shillings

Hal   Well then, once in my days I'll be a madcap.[125]

Falstaff Why, that's well said.   130

Hal   Well, come what will, I'll tarry at home.

Falstaff By the Lord, I'll be a traitor then, when thou art king.

Hal   I care not.

Poins   Sir John, I prithee leave the prince and me alone. I will
lay him down such reasons for this adventure, that he shall go.   135

Falstaff Well, God give thee the spirit of persuasion, and him the
ears of profiting, that what thou speakest may move, and what
he hears may be believed, that the true prince may (for
recreation sake[126]) prove a false thief, for the poor abuses[127]
of the time want countenance.[128] Farewell, you shall find me 140
in Eastcheap.

Hal   Farewell the latter spring,[129] farewell all-hallown
summer![130]

EXIT FALSTAFF

Poins   Now my good sweet honey lord, ride with us
tomorrow. I have a jest to execute, that I cannot manage 145
alone. Falstaff, Bardolph, Peto, and Gadshill shall rob those
men that we have already way-laid,[131] yourself and I will not
be there. And when they have the booty, if you and I do not
rob them,[132] cut this head off from my shoulders.

Hal   How shall we part with them in setting forth? 150

125 lively/impulsive young man
126 recreation sake = the sake of recreation
127 poor abuses = shabby/paltry/mean-spirited corrupt practices
128 want countenance = lack★ moral support/credit/standing
129 the latter spring = spring at the end of life, the Indian summer of old age
130 (1) period of fine weather in late autumn, (2) beauty reappearing in old age
131 prepared to lie in wait for ("ambush")
132 Falstaff et al.

Poins   Why, we will set forth before or after them, and
   appoint[133] them a place of meeting, wherein it is at our
   pleasure to fail, and then will they adventure upon[134] the
   exploit themselves, which they shall have no sooner
155   achieved[135] but we'll set upon them.

Hal   Yea, but 'tis like[136] that they will know us by our horses,
   by our habits,[137] and by every other appointment,[138] to be
   ourselves.

Poins   Tut, our horses they shall not see, I'll tie them in the
160   wood, our vizards we will change after we leave them, and
   sirrah,[139] I have cases of buckram[140] for the nonce,[141] to
   immask[142] our noted[143] outward garments.

Hal   Yea, but I doubt they[144] will be too hard[145] for us.

Poins   Well, for[146] two of them, I know them to be as true-
165   bred[147] cowards as ever turned back. And for the third, if he
   fight longer than he sees reason, I'll forswear arms.[148] The
   virtue[149] of this jest will be the incomprehensible lies that

133 settle/arrange with
134 adventure upon = undertake, chance
135 finished, completed
136 likely
137 clothing, garments★
138 (1) equipment, gear, (2) indication
139 form of address used to inferiors and children
140 cases of buckram = bags/boxes of glue-stiffened cloth
141 for the nonce = for that exact purpose
142 disguise, cover over
143 well-known
144 doubt they = fear★ Falstaff and the others
145 strong, steadfast, difficult
146 as for
147 true-bred = thoroughbred
148 forswear arms = abandon/renounce/give up★ the use of weapons/
   fighting★
149 moral excellence, excellence, merit, power★

this same fat rogue will tell us when we meet at supper, how
thirty at least he fought with, what wards,[150] what blows,
what extremities he endured, and in the reproof[151] of this   170
lives the jest.

Hal   Well, I'll go with thee. Provide us all things necessary, and
meet me tomorrow night in Eastcheap. There I'll sup.
Farewell.

Poins   Farewell my lord.   175

EXIT POINS

Hal   I know you all, and will a while uphold[152]
The unyoked[153] humor of your idleness.[154]
Yet herein will I imitate the sun,
Who doth permit the base contagious[155] clouds
To smother up[156] his beauty from the world,   180
That[157] when he please again to be himself,
Being wanted,[158] he may be more wondered[159] at
By breaking through the foul[160] and ugly mists
Of vapors,[161] that did seem to strangle him.

---

150 defensive movements, parries
151 discrediting, shaming
152 support, maintain
153 disconnected, disjoined
154 (1) foolishness, triviality, (2) avoidance of work, laziness
155 base contagious = low/plebeian/mean/inferior*/infectious/tainted/
    noxious/foul
156 smother up = conceal, cover, suppress
157 so that
158 (1) desired, needed, (2) missed
159 marveled*
160 offensive, loathsome, dirty, gross*
161 vaporous exhalations were considered a source of many kinds of evils,
    diseases, magic, and the like

185   If all the year were playing holidays,
To sport[162] would be as tedious as to work.
But when they[163] seldom come, they wished-for come,
And nothing pleaseth[164] but rare accidents.[165]
So when this loose behavior I throw off,
190   And pay the debt I never promised,[166]
By how much better than my word I am,
By so[167] much shall I falsify[168] men's hopes,
And like bright metal on a sullen ground,[169]
My reformation[170] glitt'ring o'er[171] my fault,[172]
195   Shall show more goodly,[173] and attract more eyes
Than that which hath no foil[174] to set it off.
I'll so offend,[175] to make offense[176] a skill,
Redeeming time[177] when men think least I will.

EXIT

162 take one's pleasure, amuse/entertain oneself★
163 holidays
164 satisfies, gives pleasure
165 events, happenings (the line means:"all/everything that gives pleasure is
     what comes rarely/seldom")
166 having been *born* into royal standing
167 exactly that
168 vitiate, deceive, prove false
169 sullen ground = solemn/gloomy/dull-hued background/base/founda-
     tion
170 alteration, improvement, correction
171 glitt'ring o'er = eclipsing by its brilliance/shining
172 failings★
173 favorably, graciously, beautifully★
174 backing, setting ("thin rolled-out sheet of metal")
175 so offend = thus transgress/sin
176 (1) sin, (2) disgrace, disfavor★
177 redeeming time = regaining/reclaiming/saving★ the present moment★

SCENE 3

Windsor, the council chamber

King   My blood[1] hath been too cold and temperate,[2]
Unapt[3] to stir[4] at these indignities,[5]
And you have found[6] me, for accordingly[7]
You tread[8] upon my patience. But be sure
I will from henceforth rather be myself,   5
Mighty, and to be feared, than my condition,[9]
Which hath been smooth as oil, soft as young down,[10]
And therefore lost that title of[11] respect
Which the proud soul ne'er pays but to the proud.

Worcester Our house[12] (my sovereign liege) little deserves   10
The scourge[13] of greatness to be used on it,
And that same greatness too which our own hands
Have holp[14] to make so portly.[15]

---

1 emotions, passions
2 cold and temperate = cool/unimpassioned and self-controlled/moderate/
  forbearing
3 not readily disposed/prepared
4 (1) rouse/excite to activity, (2) fight about
5 unworthy treatment, dishonorable/contemptuous acts
6 perceived, recognized, discovered
7 (1) properly, (2) logically
8 trample
9 state of being, disposition
10 (1) young birds' first feathers, (2) under-plumage of fowls
11 title of = claim/right to
12 lineage, family, clan★
13 whip, lash★
14 helped
15 imposing, majestic, grand

Northumberland   My lord —

King   Worcester get thee gone, for I do see

15   Danger[16] and disobedience in thine eye.

O sir, your presence is too bold and peremptory,[17]

And Majesty might[18] never yet endure

The moody frontier[19] of a servant brow.

You have good leave[20] to leave us. When we need

20   Your use[21] and counsel we shall send for you.

EXIT WORCESTER

You were about to speak.

Northumberland   Yea, my good lord.

Those prisoners in your Highness' name demanded,[22]

Which Harry Percy here at Holmedon took,

Were (as[23] he says) not with such strength[24] denied

25   As is delivered[25] to your Majesty.

Either envy therefore,[26] or misprision,[27]

Is guilty of this fault, and not my son.

Hotspur   My liege, I did deny no prisoners.

But I remember when the fight was done,

---

16 mischief, rebelliousness, ungraciousness
17 decisive, self-willed, stubborn
18 can
19 forehead
20 good leave = full permission (required when leaving the presence of a
   superior)
21 employment, use
22 prisoners captured in the king's name belonged to the king
23 exactly as
24 force, vigor, decisiveness
25 said, presented★
26 (1) caused by the taking of the prisoners ("for that"), *or* (2) accordingly
27 wrongful act/omission (misPREEzeeOWN)

When I was dry[28] with rage, and extreme toil,   30
Breathless and faint, leaning upon my sword,
Came there a certain[29] lord, neat and trimly[30] dressed,
Fresh as a bridegroom, and his chin new reaped[31]
Showed[32] like a stubble[33] land at harvest home.[34]
He was perfumèd like a milliner,[35]   35
And 'twixt his finger and his thumb he held
A pouncet box,[36] which[37] ever and anon[38]
He gave his nose, and took't away again
(Who[39] therewith angry, when it next came there
Took it in snuff[40]), and still[41] he smiled and talked.   40
And as the soldiers bore dead bodies by,
He called them untaught knaves,[42] unmannerly,[43]
To bring[44] a slovenly[45] unhandsome corse[46]
Betwixt the wind and his nobility.

28 (1) lacking in sympathy / cordiality, (2) uncommunicative
29 a certain = one particular
30 neat and trimly = clean and finely / elegantly ★
31 chin new reaped = beard just clipped ("harvested")
32 looked ★
33 with stumps of grain stalks left after reaping
34 harvest home = the end of the harvest
35 seller of ribbons, buttons, etc. (British meaning)
36 pouncet box = small box with perforated lid, used for perfumes / powders
   (PAWNsit)
37 from which
38 ever and anon = regularly, continually
39 which (his nose)
40 took it in snuff = (1) took snuff (powdered tobacco), (2) took offense
41 always
42 untaught knaves = ignorant rogues / menials ★
43 impolite
44 to bring = for bringing
45 untidy, messy
46 corpse

45 With many holiday and lady terms[47]
He questioned[48] me, amongst the rest demanded
My prisoners in your Majesty's behalf. [49]
I then, all smarting with[50] my wounds being cold,
To be so pestered with a popinjay,[51]
50 Out of my grief and my impatience[52]
Answered neglectingly, I know not what
He should, or he should not, for he made me mad
To see him shine so brisk,[53] and smell so sweet,
And talk so like a waiting[54] gentlewoman
55 Of guns, and drums, and wounds, God save the mark![55]
And telling me the sovereignest[56] thing on earth
Was parmacitie,[57] for an inward bruise,[58]
And that it was great pity, so it was,
This[59] villainous[60] saltpeter[61] should be digged
60 Out of the bowels of the harmless[62] earth,
Which many a good tall[63] fellow had destroyed

47 words, expressions★
48 (1) asked questions of, (2) talked to/at
49 my PRIsoNERS in your MAjesTY'S beHALF
50 smarting with = feeling sharp pain because of
51 empty, brightly decorated fop (popinjay: parrot)
52 imPAseeENCE
53 (1) finely dressed, (2) cheery, lively
54 attendant
55 God save the mark: expression of impatient scorn
56 most supreme, best
57 spermaceti: ointment made from sperm whale fat (SPERmaCIty, PARmaCIty)
58 inward bruise = internal injury/wound /contusion
59 that this
60 infamous, wicked, wretched, vile★
61 sodium nitrate, chief component of gunpowder
62 innocent
63 decent, handsome, brave★

So cowardly, and but for these vile[64] guns
He would himself have been a soldier.
This bald unjointed chat[65] of his (my lord)
I answered indirectly[66] (as I said),   65
And I beseech you, let not his report
Come current[67] for an accusation[68]
Betwixt my love and your high Majesty.

Blunt The[69] circumstance considered, good my lord,
What'er Lord Harry Percy then had said   70
To such a person, and in such a place,
At such a time, with all the rest retold,
May reasonably die, and never rise
To do him wrong, or any way impeach[70]
What then he said, so[71] he unsay it now.   75

King Why yet he doth deny his prisoners,
But with proviso and exception[72]
That we at our own charge[73] shall[74] ransom straight[75]
His brother-in-law, the foolish Mortimer,
Who on my soul hath willfully betrayed   80
The lives of those that he did lead to fight

64 disgusting, base★
65 bald unjointed chat = paltry/meager/trivial disconnected prattle/chatter/
   talk★
66 irrelevantly
67 come current = come to be/become authentic/genuine/accepted★
68 ACcyuZAseeOWN
69 with the
70 challenge, discredit
71 as long as
72 proviso and exception = conditions/stipulations and exclusions/objections
   (ekSEPseeOWN)
73 burden, expense
74 (1) must, (2) will
75 immediately

Against that great magician,[76] damned Glendower,
Whose daughter (as we hear) that Earl of March[77]
Hath lately[78] married. Shall our coffers[79] then
85   Be emptied, to redeem a traitor home?
Shall we buy treason? And indent[80] with fears[81]
When they have lost[82] and forfeited themselves?[83]
No. On the barren mountains let him starve.
For I shall never hold that man my friend
90   Whose tongue shall ask me for one penny cost[84]
To ransom home revolted Mortimer.

Hotspur Revolted Mortimer?
He never did fall off,[85] my sovereign liege,
But by the chance of war. To prove that true
95   Needs no more but[86] one tongue. For all those wounds,
Those mouthèd[87] wounds which valiantly he took,
When on the gentle Severn's[88] sedgy[89] bank,
In single opposition[90] hand to hand,
He did confound[91] the best part of an hour

76 sorcerer, conjuror
77 Mortimer
78 recently
79 strongboxes, money chests
80 make formal agreements
81 cowardly/treasonous fears
82 been defeated
83 forfeited themselves = violated/broken their oaths/pledges/faith
84 price
85 fall off = deviate from his course
86 no more but = no more than ("only")
87 gaping
88 river running from Wales into W England
89 marshy
90 combat
91 use up, spend

In changing hardiment[92] with great Glendower.   100
Three times they breathed,[93] and three times did they drink
(Upon agreement) of[94] swift Severn's flood,
Who then affrightèd with their bloody looks
Ran fearfully among the trembling reeds,
And hid his crisp[95] head in the hollow[96] bank,   105
Blood-stainèd with these valiant combatants.
Never did bare and rotten policy[97]
Color[98] her working with such deadly wounds,
Nor never could the noble Mortimer
Receive so many, and all willingly.   110
Then let not him be slandered with[99] revolt.

King Thou dost belie[100] him Percy, thou dost belie him,
He never did encounter[101] with Glendower.
I tell thee, he durst as well have met the Divel alone,
As Owen Glendower for an enemy.   115
Art thou not ashamed? But sirrah, henceforth
Let me not hear you speak of Mortimer.
Send me your prisoners with[102] the speediest means,
Or you shall hear in such a kind[103] from me

92 changing hardiment = exchanging boldness/deeds of daring
93 stopped, by agreement, to rest for a few moments
94 from
95 rippling, curled
96 empty, lean
97 expediency, craftiness, cunning
98 paint, represent, disguise
99 with the accusation/charge of
100 tell lies about, misrepresent, counterfeit
101 meet in battle, confront, fight against
102 by
103 manner, fashion

120 As will displease you. My Lord Northumberland:
We license[104] your departure with your son.
Send us your prisoners, or you will hear of it.

EXIT KING

Hotspur   And if[105] the Divel come and roar for them
I will not send them. I will after straight[106]
125 And tell him so, for I will[107] ease my heart,
Albeit[108] I make a hazard of[109] my head.
Northumberland What? Drunk with choler?[110] Stay[111] and
pause a while,
Here comes your uncle.

ENTER WORCESTER

Hotspur   Speak of Mortimer?
Zounds I will speak of him, and let my soul
130 Want mercy, if I do not join[112] with him.
Yea on his part,[113] I'll empty all these veins,
And shed my dear blood, drop by drop in the dust,
But I will lift the down-trod Mortimer
As high in the air as this unthankful king,
135 As this ingrate and cankered[114] Bolingbroke.[115]

104 grant permission for
105 and if = even if
106 will after straight = go directly after him
107 wish to
108 even though ("all be it," and so pronounced, with "be" stressed)
109 make a hazard of = take a chance / gamble with
110 temper, anger★
111 stop
112 ally myself
113 Folio: behalf
114 infected, venomous, malignant, depraved
115 the King

Northumberland Brother, the King hath made your nephew
    mad.[116]

Worcester   Who struck this heat up after I was gone?

Hotspur   He will forsooth have[117] all my prisoners,
    And when I urged[118] the ransom once again
    Of my wife's brother, then his cheek[119] looked pale,   140
    And on my face he turned an eye of death,
    Trembling even at the name of Mortimer.

Worcester   I cannot blame him. Was not he[120] proclaimed,
    By Richard[121] that dead is, the next of blood?[122]

Northumberland He was, I heard the proclamation.[123]   145
    And then it was, when the unhappy[124] king,
    (Whose wrongs in us[125] God pardon) did set forth
    Upon his Irish expedition.[126]
    From whence he, intercepted,[127] did return
    To be deposed, and shortly murderèd.   150

Worcester   And for whose death, we in the world's wide[128]
    mouth
    Live scandalized[129] and foully spoken of.

---

116 frenzied, insane
117 will forsooth have = wants in truth/indeed★ to have
118 brought forward, presented, pressed★
119 face
120 Mortimer
121 Richard II, Henry IV's predecessor
122 kin
123 PRAclaMAseeOWN
124 miserable, unlucky, unfortunate
125 whose wrongs in us = the wrongs against whom by us
126 EXpeDIseeOWN
127 cut off, stopped on the way
128 (1) big, loose, (2) wide open
129 shamed, disgraced

Hotspur   But soft,[130] I pray[131] you. Did King Richard then

Proclaim my brother[132] Edmund Mortimer

Heir to the crown?

155 Northumberland   He did, myself did hear it.

Hotspur   Nay then I cannot blame his cousin king,

That wished him on the barren mountains starve.[133]

But shall[134] it be that you that set the crown

Upon the head of this forgetful man,[135]

160 And for his sake wear the detested blot[136]

Of murderous subornation?[137] Shall it be

That you a world of curses undergo,

Being the agents,[138] or base second[139] means,

The cords,[140] the ladder, or the hangman rather?

165 O pardon me, that I descend so low,

To show the line[141] and the predicament[142]

Wherein you range[143] under this subtle[144] king!

Shall it for shame be spoken in these days,

---

130 but soft = just a minute★
131 ask, request★
132 relatives by marriage were commonly termed blood kinfolk
133 to starve
134 (1) must, (2) will
135 the King —
136 stain, spot
137 arranging for someone to do something evil (SUborNAYshun)
138 instruments, employees
139 inferior, secondary
140 ropes
141 boundaries, limits
142 difficult/dangerous position
143 wherein you range = where you are set/arranged, which you occupy
144 elusive, clever, dexterous

Or fill up chronicles[145] in time to come,

That men of your nobility and power   170

Did gage them both[146] in an unjust behalf[147]

(As both of you, God pardon it, have done)

To put down Richard, that sweet lovely rose,

And plant this thorn, this canker[148] Bolingbroke?

And shall it in more shame be further spoken   175

That you are fooled, discarded, and shook off

By him, for whom these shames ye underwent?

No, yet time serves,[149] wherein you may redeem

Your banished honors,[150] and restore yourselves

Into the good thoughts of the world again.[151]   180

Revenge the jeering and disdained[152] contempt

Of this proud king, who studies[153] day and night

To answer[154] all the debt he owes to you,

Even with the bloody payment of your deaths.

Therefore I say —

Worcester   Peace[155] cousin, say no more.   185

And now I will unclasp[156] a secret book,

145 historical records★
146 gage them both = pledge/mortgage/undertake, both of you
147 side, cause★
148 ulcer, gangrenous sore
149 yet time serves = there is still time left
150 your banished honors = your (plural) dismissed/exiled personal honor
151 inTO the GOOD thoughts OF the WORLD aGAIN
152 jeering and disdained = mocking/scoffing and scornful
153 applies himself, thinks, deliberates
154 to answer = how to meet/respond to/pay off/satisfy
155 be silent★
156 open

And to your quick-conceiving discontents[157]
I'll read you matter[158] deep and dangerous,[159]
As full of peril and adventurous[160] spirit,
190   As to o'er-walk a current[161] roaring loud
On the unsteadfast footing[162] of a spear.

Hotspur   If he fall in, goodnight, or[163] sink, or swim.
Send danger from the east unto the west,
So[164] honor cross it from the north to south,
195   And let them[165] grapple.[166] O the blood more stirs
To rouse a lion than to start a hare.

Northumberland Imagination of some great exploit
Drives him beyond the bounds of patience.

Hotspur   By heaven methinks it were an easy leap
200   To pluck bright honor from the pale-faced moon,
Or dive into the bottom of the deep,
Where fathom-line[167] could never touch the ground,
And pluck up drownèd honor by the locks,
So he that doth redeem her thence[168] might wear
205   Without co-rival[169] all her dignities.

---

157 quick-conceiving discontents = rapidly understood/imagined/thought-
    of dissatisfactions/vexations
158 substance, material
159 (1) hard, difficult, delicate, (2) perilous, hurtful★
160 risky, daring, rash
161 stream
162 unsteadfast footing = shaky/unsteady support/foundation
163 whether (or . . . or = either . . . or)
164 as long as
165 danger and honor
166 wrestle, fight
167 weighted rope used to determine water depth
168 her thence = honor from there
169 any equal competitor★

But out upon[170] this half-faced fellowship.[171]

Worcester He apprehends[172] a world of figures[173] here,

But not the form[174] of what he should attend.[175]

Good cousin, give me audience[176] for a while.

Hotspur I cry you mercy.[177]   210

Worcester Those same noble Scots that are your

prisoners –

Hotspur I'll keep them all.

By God he shall not have a Scot[178] of them.

No, if a Scot[179] would[180] save his soul he shall not.

I'll keep them, by this hand.

Worcester   You start away,[181]   215

And lend no ear unto my purposes.

Those prisoners you shall keep.

Hotspur Nay, I will. That's flat.[182]

He said he would not ransom *Mortimer,*

Forbade my tongue to speak of *Mortimer,*   220

But I will find him when he lies asleep,

And in his ear I'll holla[183] *Mortimer,*

---

170 out upon = down with

171 half-faced fellowship = imperfect/half-and-half sharing/participation

172 perceives, feels

173 shapes, forms

174 structure, character

175 should attend = ought to listen/turn his attention/mind to★

176 your attention ("listening")

177 cry you mercy = beg your pardon★

178 (1) Scotsman, (2) small payment/contribution

179 (1) Scotsman, (2) small payment/contribution

180 might

181 start away = jump back

182 plain, absolute, downright

183 shout (call to hunting dogs)

Nay, I'll have a starling shall be taught to speak[184]

Nothing but *Mortimer,* and give it him[185]

225   To keep his anger still in motion.[186]

Worcester   Hear you cousin. A word.

Hotspur   All studies[187] here I solemnly defy,[188]

Save how to gall and pinch[189] this Bolingbroke,

And that same sword-and-buckler[190] Prince of Wales.

230   But[191] that I think his father loves him not,

And would be glad he met with some mischance,[192]

I would have him poisoned with a pot[193] of ale.

Worcester   Farewell kinsman, I'll talk to you

When you are better tempered[194] to attend.

235 *Northumberland* Why what a wasp-stung and impatient fool

Art thou, to break into this woman's mood,

Tying[195] thine ear to no tongue but thine own?

Hotspur   Why look you, I am whipped and scourged

with rods,[196]

Nettled,[197] and stung with pismires,[198] when I hear

184 say

185 give it him = give the starling to him

186 still in motion = always active

187 desires, longings, interests

188 renounce, declare hostility toward / war on, challenge★

189 gall and pinch = annoy / harass / oppress and squeeze / nip

190 sword-and-buckler = bragging, blustering (buckler = small round shield)★

191 except

192 disaster★ (missCHANCE)

193 container

194 better tempered = in the right / proper frame of mind

195 binding, constricting

196 sticks

197 beaten / stung by nettles (prickly shrubs)

198 with pismires = by ants (PIZZmires)

Of this vile politician[199] Bolingbroke,   240

In Richard's time – what do you call the place?

A plague upon it, it is[200] in Gloucestershire[201] –

'Twas where the madcap[202] duke his uncle kept,[203]

His uncle York, where I first bowed my knee

Unto this king of smiles, this Bolingbroke.   245

'Sblood, when you and he came back from Ravenspurgh.[204]

Northumberland At Berkeley[205] castle.

Hotspur   You say true.[206]

Why what a candy deal[207] of courtesy[208]

This fawning greyhound[209] then did profer[210] me.

"Look when[211] his infant fortune[212] came to age,"[213]   250

And "gentle Harry Percy," and "kind cousin."

O the Devil take such cozeners.[214] (*to Worcester*) God forgive me,

Good uncle tell your tale, I have done.

Worcester   Nay, if you have not, to it[215] again,

199 schemer, plotter, intriguer
200 IT'S
201 county in SW England (GLAStiSHIR)
202 reckless, wildly impulsive
203 stayed at, dwelled
204 a harbor in Yorkshire, N England
205 BARklee
206 you say true = that's right
207 candy deal = sugary lot/quantity★
208 polite manners★
209 "large dog"
210 present/say to
211 look when = just see how
212 infant fortune = early/childhood success/good luck
213 came to age = has grown up
214 deceivers, impostors
215 to it = go to it

We will stay[216] your leisure.

255 *Hotspur*   I have done, i'faith.

Worcester Then once more to your Scottish prisoners.

Deliver[217] them up without their ransom straight,

And make the Douglas' son[218] your only mean[219]

For powers[220] in Scotland. Which for divers[221] reasons

260 Which I shall send you written, be assured

Will easily be granted. (*to Northumberland*) You my lord,

Your son in Scotland being thus employed,

Shall secretly into the bosom creep

Of that same[222] noble prelate[223] well-beloved,

The Archbishop.

Hotspur   Of York, is it not?

265 *Worcester*   True, who bears hard[224]

His brother's death at Bristow, the lord Scroop.[225]

I speak not this in estimation,[226]

As what I think might be, but what I know

Is ruminated,[227] plotted,[228] and set down,

270 And only stays but to behold the face

Of that occasion[229] that shall bring it on.

216 await
217 set free, release
218 Mordake, Earl of Fife
219 intermediary, agent, intercessor
220 armies
221 various, sundry
222 identical, exact
223 high-ranking church dignitary
224 with great difficulty
225 Earl of Wiltshire, executed by Henry IV at Bristow, in 1399
226 conjecture, guess (EStiMAseeOWN)
227 considered
228 planned
229 opportunity★

Hotspur	I smell it. Upon my life it will do well.
Northumberland	Before the game[230] is afoot[231] thou still let'st slip.[232]
Hotspur	Why, it cannot choose but be a noble plot.

And then the power of Scotland, and of York,   275
To join with Mortimer, ha?

Worcester	And so they shall.
Hotspur	In faith it is exceedingly well aimed.[233]
Worcester	And 'tis no little reason bids us speed,

To save our heads by raising of a head.[234]
For, bear ourselves as even[235] as we can,   280
The King will always think him[236] in our debt,
And think we think ourselves unsatisfied,[237]
Till he hath found a time to pay us home.[238]
And see already how he doth begin
To make us strangers to his looks of love.   285

Hotspur	He does, he does, we'll be revenged on him.
Worcester	Cousin, farewell. No further go in this

Than I by letters shall direct your course.
When time is ripe, which will be suddenly,[239]
I'll steal to Glendower, and Lord Mortimer,   290

---

230 (1) sport, contest, (2) hunt
231 in process/operation, active
232 still let'st slip = always allow it to escape/get away/leak out (hounds are slipped when freed from their leashes)
233 considered, calculated, planned
234 force, army
235 steadily
236 himself
237 (1) unpaid, (2) dissatisfied
238 pay us home = pay off/back
239 (1) very soon, (2) happen abruptly

Where you, and Douglas, and our powers at once,[240]
As I will fashion[241] it, shall happily[242] meet,
To bear our fortunes in our own strong arms,
Which[243] now we hold at[244] much uncertainty.

295 *Northumberland* Farewell good brother, we shall thrive,[245]
I trust.

Hotspur　　　　　Uncle adieu. O let the hours be short
Till fields,[246] and blows, and groans, applaud our sport.[247]

EXEUNT

240 at once = together
241 (1) contrive, manage, (2) prosper, flourish★
242 successfully, fortunately
243 which fortunes/destinies
244 hold at = maintain/guard with
245 flourish, prosper, be successful
246 battlefields
247 entertainment, diversion ("fun and games")

Act 2

SCENE I

Rochester. An Inn Yard

ENTER A CARRIER WITH A LANTERN IN HIS HAND

Carrier 1 Heigh ho. An it be not four by the day,[1] I'll be hanged.
   Charles' wain[2] is over the new chimney, and yet our horse not
   packed.[3] What, Ostler!

Ostler (within) Anon,[4] anon.

Carrier 1 I prithee, Tom,[5] beat[6] Cut's saddle, put a few flocks[7] in   5
   the point.[8] The poor jade[9] is wrung in the withers,[10] out of
   all cess.[11]

1 by the day = in the morning
2 group of seven bright stars in the Great Bear constellation (wain = chariot,
   wagon)
3 loaded
4 straightaway, immediately*
5 the ostler
6 soften / shape by beating
7 tufts of wool
8 pommel (protuberant front part of a saddle)
9 worn-out draught horse
10 wrung in the withers = being squeezed / pressed on the high part of the
   back, between the shoulder blades
11 out of all cess = constantly

ENTER CARRIER 2

Carrier 2 Peas and beans[12] are as dank[13] here[14] as a dog,[15] and
    that is the next[16] way to give poor jades the bots.[17] This
10   house[18] is turned upside down since Robin Ostler died.

Carrier 1 Poor fellow never joyed[19] since the price of oats rose, it
    was the death of him.

Carrier 2 I think this be the most villainous house in all London
    road[20] for fleas. I am stung like a tench.[21]

15 *Carrier 1* Like a tench! By the mass there is ne'er a king in
    Christendom[22] could be better bit than I have been since the
    first cock.[23]

Carrier 2 Why, they will allow us ne'er a jordan,[24] and then we
    leak[25] in your chimney,[26] and your chamber-lye[27] breeds
20   fleas like a loach.[28]

Carrier 1 What, Ostler! Come away[29] and be hanged, come
    away!

12 food for animals as well as for men
13 watery
14 at this inn
15 a derisive negative of no precise meaning
16 shortest, most direct
17 maggots
18 inn
19 was happy
20 London road = the road to London
21 like a tench = so that I look like a red-spotted fish
22 Folio; Quarto: king christen
23 cock-crow
24 chamber pot
25 urinate
26 your chimney = the fireplace
27 chamber-lye = urine
28 quick-breeding fish
29 come away = get on with it, come on out here

Carrier 2 I have a gammon[30] of bacon, and two razes[31] of
    ginger, to be delivered as far as Charing Cross.[32]

Carrier 1 God's body, the turkeys in my pannier are quite   25
    starved. What, Ostler? A plague on thee, hast thou never an
    eye in thy head? Canst not hear? And[33] t'were not as good
    deed as drink,[34] to break the pate on thee,[35] I am[36] a very
    villain. Come and be hanged! Hast no faith in thee?

ENTER GADSHILL

Gadshill Good morrow, carriers. What's o'clock?   30

Carrier 1 I think it be two o'clock.

Gadshill I prithee lend me thy lantern, to see[37] my gelding in
    the stable.

Carrier 1 Nay by God, soft! I know a trick worth two of that,[38]
    i'faith.   35

Gadshill (*to Carrier 2*) I pray thee lend me thine.

Carrier 2 Ay, when? Canst tell? Lend me thy lantern, quoth[39] he.
    Marry, I'll see thee hanged first.

Gadshill Sirrah Carrier, what time do you mean[40] to come to[41]
    London?   40

30 ham, haunch
31 roots
32 on the far side of London
33 and if
34 good deed as drink = good a deed as drinking (which of course is very
    good indeed)
35 break the pate on thee = crack open your head
36 may be called
37 find, identify
38 I'm not a fool (proverbial)
39 says
40 intend
41 come to = reach, arrive in

Carrier 2 Time enough to go to bed with a candle,[42] I warrant[43]
thee. Come neighbor Mugs, we'll call up[44] the gentlemen.[45]
They will along with[46] company, for they have great
charge.[47]

EXEUNT CARRIERS

ENTER CHAMBERLAIN

45 **Gadshill**   What ho, Chamberlain?

   Chamberlain At hand,[48] quoth pickpurse.[49]

   Gadshill   That's even as fair[50] as "at hand, quoth the
chamberlain." For thou variest[51] no more from picking of
purses, than giving direction[52] doth from laboring. Thou

50   layest the plot how.

   Chamberlain Good morrow, master[53] Gadshill. It holds current
that[54] I told you yesternight. There's a franklin[55] in[56] the
Weald[57] of Kent hath brought three hundred marks[58] with
him, in gold. I heard him tell it to one of his company last

42 i.e., after sunset
43 promise, guarantee★
44 call up = awaken
45 i.e., other less plebeian travelers, lodging that night at the inn
46 will along with = will want to go along/travel with
47 great charge = a lot to carry
48 here I am, I'm close by
49 pickpocket
50 even as fair = just★ as plausible
51 differ, diverge
52 ordering, commanding, instructing
53 mister
54 holds current that = remains up-to-date/true that which
55 upper-middle-class landholder
56 of, from
57 wilderness, wood (WILD)
58 (1) large coins, originally of silver, (2) weight of roughly half a pound

night at supper, a kind of auditor, one that hath abundance of   55
charge too, God knows what. They are up already, and call for
eggs and butter. They will away[59] presently.[60]

Gadshill   Sirrah, if they meet not with Saint Nicholas'
clerks,[61] I'll give thee this neck.[62]

Chamberlain No, I'll[63] none of it. I pray thee keep that for the   60
hangman, for I know thou worshippest Saint Nicholas, as
truly as a man of falsehood may.

Gadshill   What talkest thou to me of the hangman? If I hang,
I'll make[64] a fat pair of gallows. For if I hang, old Sir John
hangs with me, and thou knowest he is no starveling.[65] Tut,   65
there are other Trojans[66] that thou dreamst not of, the which
for sport sake are content to do the profession some grace,[67]
that would (if matters should be looked into) for their own
credit[68] sake make all whole. I am joined with no foot-
landrakers,[69] no long-staff sixpenny strikers,[70] none of these   70
mad mustachio purple-hued maltworms,[71] but with nobility,

---

59 will away = (1) wish to leave, (2) will leave
60 soon, without delay★
61 Saint Nicholas' clerks = highwaymen, robbers (St. Nicholas: patron saint of
   travelers)
62 i.e., to be hanged
63 I'll = I will = I want
64 cause the making of
65 starved/emaciated person
66 good fellows, drinkers, carousers
67 honor
68 credit = credit's = reputation's
69 foot-landrakers = footpads = highwaymen who operate on foot rather than
   on horseback
70 long-staff sixpenny strikers = long-cudgeled paltry/petty vagrants
71 purple-hued maltworms = purple-faced topers (drinkers wild for malt
   liquor)

and tranquility, burgomasters[72] and great oners,[73] such as can
hold in,[74] such as will strike sooner than speak, and speak
sooner than drink, and drink sooner than pray, and yet
75   (zounds!) I lie, for they pray continually to their saint the
Commonwealth,[75] or rather not pray to her, but prey on her,
for they ride up and down on her, and make her their
boots.[76]

Chamberlain What, the Commonwealth their boots? Will she
80   hold[77] out water in foul way?[78]

Gadshill   She will, she will, justice[79] hath liquored her.[80] We
steal as[81] in a castle cocksure.[82] We have the receipt[83] of
fern-seed,[84] we walk invisible.

Chamberlain Nay by my faith, I think you are more beholding[85]
85   to the night than to fern-seed, for your walking invisible.

Gadshill   Give me thy hand, thou shalt have a share in our
purchase,[86] as I am a true man.

---

72 magistrates (burg = town)
73 unique/remarkable ones ("one-ers": slang)
74 hold in = keep secrets/their mouths shut
75 the nation as a whole
76 plunder ("booty")
77 keep
78 foul way = (1) *literally:* a muddy/wet road, (2) *metaphorically:* protect you in
    need
79 i.e., the persons in charge of administering the law
80 liquored her = (1) made her drunk, (2) greased her
81 as if
82 absolutely safe
83 formula, recipe
84 fern-seed = ferns were thought to reproduce via invisible seeds; anyone
    swallowing that seed would thus become invisible
85 indebted, obliged ("beholden")
86 plunder, pillage

Chamberlain Nay, rather let me have it,[87] as you are a false thief.

Gadshill   Go to, *homo* is a common name to all men.[88] Bid
the ostler bring my gelding out of the stable. Farewell, you   90
muddy[89] knave.

EXEUNT

87 a share
88 *homo* (Latin) = man, whether honest or not (possibly alluding to a 1549
    grammar, defining a noun as either "proper" or else "common to all men")
89 muddled, dull-witted

SCENE 2

The highway near Gad's Hill

ENTER HAL, POINS, PETO, AND BARDOLPH

Poins   Come shelter,[1] shelter, I have removed[2] Falstaff's horse,
and he[3] frets[4] like a gummed velvet.[5]

Hal   Stand close.[6]

THEY STEP TO ONE SIDE

ENTER FALSTAFF

Falstaff Poins, Poins, and be hanged! Poins!

5 *Hal* (*coming forward*) Peace, ye fat-kidneyed rascal, what a
brawling[7] dost thou keep![8]

Falstaff Where's Poins, Hal?

Hal   He is walked up to the top of the hill. I'll go seek him.

EXIT HAL

Falstaff I am accursed[9] to rob in that thief's company. The rascal
10   hath removed my horse, and tied him I know not where. If I
travel but four foot by the squier[10] further afoot, I shall break
my wind.[11] Well, I doubt not but to die a fair death for all

1 (verb) hide
2 move, shifted the location of
3 Falstaff
4 (1) worries, is anxious, (2) is consumed, worn away
5 gummed velvet = quickly worn-out velvet cloth made to look better by the
application of resin / tree sap
6 stand close = step back / out of sight★
7 clamor, indecent noise
8 maintain, employ, practice
9 doomed
10 rule, measure ("square")
11 break my wind = exhaust / ruin my breath / breathing

this, if I scape hanging for killing that rogue. I have forsworn
his company hourly any time this two and twenty years, and
yet I am bewitched[12] with the rogue's company. If the rascal   15
have not given me medicines[13] to make me love him, I'll be
hanged. It could not be else, I have drunk medicines. Poins,
Hal, a plague upon you both! Bardolph, Peto, I'll starve[14] ere
I'll rob a foot further! And[15] 'twere not as good a deed as
drink to turn true man, and to leave these rogues, I am the   20
veriest varlet[16] that ever chewed with a tooth. Eight yards of
uneven ground is threescore and ten miles afoot with me, and
the stony-hearted villains know it well enough. A plague
upon it when thieves cannot be true one to another!

THEY WHISTLE

Whew, a plague upon you all. Give me my horse you rogues,   25
give me my horse and be hanged!

Hal   (*coming forward*) Peace ye fat guts, lie down, lay thine ear
close to the ground, and list if thou canst hear the tread[17] of
travelers.

Falstaff   Have you any levers to lift me up again, being down?   30
'Sblood, I'll not bear mine own flesh so far afoot again for all
the coin in thy father's exchequer.[18] What a plague mean ye
to colt[19] me thus?

---

12 (1) compelled by magical influence, (2) fascinated
13 potions
14 die (compare German *sterben*)
15 if
16 veriest varlet = truest rogue/rascal★
17 steps ((horses'))
18 treasury
19 cheat, take in, fool

	Hal	Thou liest, thou art not colted, thou art uncolted.[20]
35	*Falstaff*	I prithee good prince Hal, help me to[21] my horse, good king's son.
	Hal	Out ye rogue, shall I be your ostler?
	Falstaff	Hang thyself in thine own heir-apparent garters![22] If I be ta'en, I'll peach[23] for this. And[24] I have not ballads made
40		on[25] you all, and sung to filthy[26] tunes, let a cup of sack be my poison. When a jest is so forward,[27] and afoot too! I hate it.

ENTER GADSHILL

	Gadshill	Stand.
	Falstaff	So I do, against my will.
45	*Poins*	O 'tis our setter,[28] I know his voice. Bardolph, what news?
	Bardolph	Case[29] ye, case ye. On with your vizards, there's money of the King's coming down the hill, 'tis going to the King's exchequer.
50	*Falstaff*	You lie, ye rogue, 'tis going to the King's tavern.
	Gadshill	There's enough to make[30] us all.
	Falstaff	To be hanged.

20 deprived of a horse / colt
21 get
22 the heir apparent to the throne became by right a member of the Order of the Garter, the highest order of English knighthood
23 inform against, betray
24 if
25 about
26 nasty, obscene, disgraceful, scurvy
27 early, ahead of its time★
28 person spying on potential victims
29 cover
30 to make = to be the making of

Hal   Sirs, you four shall front[31] them in the narrow lane.
    Ned Poins and I will walk lower. If they scape from your
    encounter,[32] then they light on[33] us.   55

Peto   How many be there of them?

Gadshill Some eight or ten.

Falstaff Zounds, will they not rob us?

Hal   What, a coward, Sir John Paunch?

Falstaff Indeed, I am not John of Gaunt, your grandfather, but   60
    yet no coward, Hal.

Hal   Well, we leave that to the proof.

Poins   Sirrah Jack, thy horse stands behind the hedge. When
    thou needst him, there thou shalt find him. Farewell and
    stand fast.   65

Falstaff Now cannot I strike him,[34] if I should be[35] hanged.

Hal   (*aside to Poins*) Ned, where are our disguises?

Poins   (*aside*) Here, hard by, stand close.

EXEUNT HAL AND POINS

Falstaff Now my masters,[36] happy man be his dole,[37] say I.
    Every man to his business.   70

ENTER TRAVELERS

Traveler 1 Come neighbor, the boy shall lead our horses down
    the hill. We'll walk afoot a while and ease our legs.

31 confront
32 face-to-face meeting
33 light on = descend/proceed to, fall/arrive on
34 strike him = reach the horse
35 should be = must be/am going to be
36 comrades, fellow workmen
37 happy man be his dole = may happiness be our destiny/fate (proverbial)

Thieves   Stand!

Traveler 2   Jesus bless us!

75 *Falstaff*   Strike, down with them, cut the villains' throats! Ah
whoreson[38] caterpillars, bacon-fed knaves, they hate us
youth! Down with them, fleece[39] them.

Traveler 1   O, we are undone,[40] both we and ours for ever.

Falstaff   Hang ye, gorbellied[41] knaves, are ye undone? No, ye
80 fat chuffs,[42] I would your store[43] were here. On, bacons, on!
What, ye knaves! Young men must live. You are grand
jurors,[44] are ye? We'll jure[45] ye, faith!

THEY ROB AND BIND THEM. EXEUNT

ENTER HAL AND POINS

Hal   The thieves have bound the true[46] men. Now could
thou and I rob the thieves, and go merrily to London, it
85 would be argument[47] for a week, laughter for a month, and a
good jest for ever.

Poins   Stand close, I hear them coming.

HAL AND POINS STEP TO THE SIDE

ENTER THIEVES

Falstaff   Come, my masters, let us share,[48] and then to horse

38 (1) bastard, (2) vile, wretched, disgusting
39 strip (as wool is clipped off sheep)
40 ruined, destroyed
41 corpulent, fat-bellied
42 (1) misers, (2) clowns
43 would your store = wish your abundance / goods
44 grand jurors = important / wealthy men were selected as grand jurors
45 make jurors of
46 honest
47 topic of discussion / conversation
48 divide up

before day. And[49] the Prince and Poins be not two arrant[50]
cowards there's no equity stirring.[51] There's no more valor[52]   90
in that Poins than in a wild duck.

AS THEY ARE SHARING, HAL AND POINS SET UPON THEM

Hal   Your money!
Poins   Villains!

THE OTHERS RUN AWAY. AFTER A BLOW OR TWO,
FALSTAFF RUNS, TOO, LEAVING THE BOOTY BEHIND

Hal   Got with much ease. Now merrily to horse. The
thieves are all scattered, and possessed with fear so strongly   95
that they dare not meet each other. Each takes his fellow for
an officer. Away good Ned. Falstaff sweats to death, and
lards[53] the lean[54] earth as he walks along. Wer't not for
laughing, I should pity him.
Poins   How the rogue roared.   100

EXEUNT

49 if
50 downright, unmitigated
51 equity stirring = fairness/justice in the world (stirring = alive/moving)
52 (1) bravery, courage, (2) merit
53 drips fat on ("bastes")
54 meager ("not fat")

SCENE 3
Warkworth Castle[1]

ENTER HOTSPUR, READING A LETTER

Hotspur *But for mine own part, my Lord, I could be well contented
to be there, in respect of* [2] *the love I bear your house.* He could be
contented: why is he not then? In the respect of the love he
bears our house: he shows in this, he loves his own barn better
than he loves our house. Let me see some more. *The purpose
you undertake is dangerous.* Why, that's certain. 'Tis dangerous
to take[3] a cold, to sleep, to drink, but I tell you (my Lord fool)
out of this nettle "danger," we pluck this flower "safety." *The
purpose you undertake is dangerous, the friends you have named
uncertain, the time itself unsorted,* [4] *and your whole plot too light,* [5]
for the counterpoise of [6] *so great an opposition.* Say you so, say you
so? I say unto you again, you are a shallow cowardly hind,[7]
and you lie. What a lack-brain is this! By the Lord, our plot is
a good plot, as[8] ever was laid,[9] our friends true and constant.
A good plot, good friends, and full of expectation![10] An
excellent plot, very good friends! What a frosty-spirited rogue
is this! Why, my Lord of York commends the plot, and the

1 the seat/principal residence of the Percy family, in Northumberland
2 in respect of = for
3 "catch"
4 (1) unsuitable, unfitted, (2) unsettled, disordered
5 deficient, light-weighted
6 for the counterpoise of = to be balanced against
7 field hand, farm servant
8 as good as
9 set, brought to light
10 anticipation, reason for expecting profit

general course[11] of the action.[12] Zounds, and[13] I were now
by[14] this rascal I could brain him with his lady's fan. Is there
not my father, my uncle, and myself? Lord Edmund   20
Mortimer, my Lord of York, and Owen Glendower? Is there
not besides the Douglas? Have I not all their letters to meet
me in arms[15] by the ninth of the next month, and are they
not some of them set[16] forward already? What a pagan rascal
is this, an infidel! Ha, you shall see now in very sincerity of   25
fear and cold heart, will he[17] to the King, and lay open all our
proceedings! O, I could divide myself,[18] and go to buffets,[19]
for moving[20] such a dish of skim milk with so honorable an
action. Hang him, let him tell the King, we are prepared. I
will set forward tonight.   30

ENTER LADY PERCY

How now, Kate, I must leave you within these two hours.
Kate O my good lord,[21] why are you thus alone?
For what offense have I this fortnight been
A banished woman from my Harry's bed?
Tell me (sweet lord) what is't that takes from thee   35

11 general course = whole/entire* direction, path
12 deed, event, operation*
13 if
14 close to, beside
15 in arms = ready to fight
16 started
17 will he = he will go
18 divide myself = separate/cut myself into two
19 blows, fighting (BUFfts)*
20 proposing, prompting
21 husband

Thy stomach,[22] pleasure, and thy golden[23] sleep?
Why dost thou bend thine eyes upon the earth,
And start[24] so often when thou sit'st alone?
Why hast thou lost the fresh blood in thy cheeks,
40 And given my treasures and my rights of thee
To thick-eyed[25] musing, and curst[26] melancholy?
In thy faint[27] slumbers I by thee have watched,
And heard thee murmur tales of iron[28] wars,
Speak terms of manage[29] to thy bounding steed,
45 Cry "Courage! To the field!"[30] And thou hast talked
Of sallies, and retires,[31] of trenches, tents,
Of palisadoes,[32] frontiers,[33] parapets,[34]
Of basilisks,[35] of cannon, culverin,[36]
Of prisoners' ransom, and of soldiers slain,
50 And all the currents[37] of a heady[38] fight.
Thy spirit within thee hath been so at war,

22 (1) appetite (for food), (2) inclination, desire (for other things)
23 precious, important, most excellent
24 flinch, recoil
25 thick-eyed = excessive, heavy, profound
26 detestable, cantankerous, shrewish
27 languid, feeble, sluggish
28 extremely hard / stern (EYErin)
29 handling, control
30 battlefield (Quarto and Folio: cry courage to the field; all editors emend –
   but all editors, including this one, may well be wrong)
31 retreats*
32 palisades (PAliSAdoes)
33 front lines
34 breast-high defenses, breastworks
35 large cannon
36 long cannon
37 movements, ebbs and flows
38 passionate, violent

And thus hath so bestirred thee in thy sleep,

That beads of sweat have stood upon thy brow

Like bubbles in a late[39] disturbèd stream,

And in thy face strange motions[40] have appeared,   55

Such as we see when men restrain their breath,

On some great sudden hest.[41] O what portents[42] are these?

Some heavy business hath my lord in hand,

And I must know it. Else he loves me not.

Hotspur (*calling*) What ho!

ENTER SERVANT

                Is[43] Gilliams with the packet[44] gone?   60

Servant   He is my Lord, an hour ago.

Hotspur   Hath Butler brought those horses from the sheriff?

Servant   One horse, my lord, he brought even[45] now.

Hotspur   What[46] horse? A roan,[47] a crop-ear,[48] is it not?

Servant   It is, my Lord.

Hotspur   That roan shall be my throne.   65

Well, I will back him[49] straight: O Esperance![50]

Bid Butler lead him forth into the park.[51]

39 recently
40 movements
41 (1) command, (2) determination
42 signs, tokens (porTENTS)
43 has
44 small package, parcel
45 just
46 what kind of
47 chestnut-colored
48 crop-ear = a cut/notched ear
49 back him = mount him, sit on his back
50 "Esperance en dieu" (I trust in God): Percy family motto★
51 grounds around a large house

	Kate	But hear you, my lord.
	Hotspur	What say'st thou, my lady?
70	Kate	What is it carries[52] you away?
	Hotspur	Why, my horse (my love), my horse.
	Kate	Out,[53] you mad-headed ape,

A weasel hath not such a deal of spleen[54]
As you are tossed with.[55] In faith
I'll know your business, Harry, that I will.
I fear my brother Mortimer doth stir[56]
About his title, and hath sent for you
To line[57] his enterprise, but if you go –

Hotspur So far afoot, I shall be weary, love.

80 *Kate*   Come, come you paraquito,[58] answer me
Directly[59] unto this question that I ask.
In faith I'll break thy little finger, Harry,
And if thou wilt not tell me all things true.[60]

Hotspur Away,

85   Away you trifler.[61] Love? I love thee not,
I care not for thee, Kate. This is no world
To play with mammets,[62] and to tilt[63] with lips.

---

52 (1) bears (physically), (2) leads (psychologically)
53 reproachful exclamation
54 deal of spleen = quantity/share of whims/caprices/temper★
55 tossed with = troubled/disturbed by
56 agitate
57 (1) arrange, (2) outline, plan, (3) reinforce, strengthen
58 little parrot
59 plainly
60 truthfully
61 joker, worthless/frivolous person
62 dolls, puppets
63 joust (fight/battle)

We must have bloody noses, and cracked crowns,[64]
And pass them current[65] too. (*calling*) God's me,[66] my horse!
What say'st thou, Kate? What wouldst thou have with me?   90

Kate   Do you not love me? Do you not indeed?
Well, do not then, for since you love me not
I will not love my self.[67] Do you not love me?
Nay, tell me if you speak in jest or no?

Hotspur Come, wilt thou see me ride?   95
And when I am a-horseback, I will swear
I love thee infinitely. But hark you[68] Kate,
I must not have you henceforth question me
Whither I go, nor reason[69] whereabout.
Whither I must, I must. And to conclude,   100
This evening must I leave you, gentle Kate.
I know you wise,[70] but yet no farther wise
Than Harry Percy's wife. Constant you are,
But yet a woman, and for secrecy
No lady closer,[71] for I well believe   105
Thou wilt not utter what thou dost not know.
And so far will I trust thee, gentle Kate.

Kate   How? So far?

Hotspur Not an inch further. But hark you Kate,
Whither I go, thither shall you go too.   110

64 (1) heads, (2) coins
65 pass them current = keep even cracked crowns in current circulation
   (cracked coins were often rejected)
66 God's me = God save me
67 either, for my part
68 hark you = listen★
69 discuss
70 prudent, sensible
71 more reserved/secret/reticent

Today will I set forth, tomorrow you.

Will this content you, Kate?

Kate   It must of force.[72]

EXEUNT

---

72 of force = simply, of necessity

SCENE 4

Eastcheap, the Boar's Head Tavern

ENTER HAL AND POINS

Hal　Ned, prithee come out of that fat[1] room, and lend me thy
hand to laugh a little.

Poins　Where hast been, Hal?

Hal　With three or four loggerheads,[2] amongst three or
fourscore hogsheads.[3] I have sounded[4] the very bass string of　　5
humility. Sirrah, I am sworn brother to a leash of drawers,[5]
and can call them all by their Christen[6] names, as Tom, Dick,
and Francis. They take it already upon their salvation,[7] that
though I be but Prince of Wales, yet I am the king of
courtesy, and tell me flatly I am no proud Jack[8] like Falstaff,　　10
but a Corinthian,[9] a lad of mettle,[10] a good boy (by the Lord
so they call me), and when I am King of England I shall
command all the good lads in Eastcheap. They call drinking
deep "dyeing scarlet,"[11] and when you breathe in your

---

1 heavy-aired, dense with odors
2 blockheads
3 fourscore hogsheads = 80 (score = 20) liquor casks of roughly 60 gallons
each (Hal has been at a drinking party held by what are now called
"bartenders," held in a wine cellar)
4 (1) uttered, made resound, (2) sunk down to, (3) plumbed
5 leash of drawers = set of three tapsters/bartenders
6 Christian
7 upon their salvation = may they be saved ("by God") (Folio: upon their
confidence)
8 (1) fellow, man, (2) knave, low-bred★ (Falstaff's name is also, of course, Jack)
9 profligate, thoroughly dissolute
10 spirit, ardor★
11 i.e., heavy drinkers are red-faced

15   watering[12] they cry "Hem!" and bid you "play[13] it off." To
     conclude, I am[14] so good a proficient[15] in one quarter of an
     hour that I can drink with any tinker[16] in his own language
     during[17] my life. I tell thee, Ned, thou hast lost much honor,
     that thou wert not with me in this action. But sweet Ned, to
20   sweeten which name of Ned, I give thee this pennyworth of
     sugar,[18] clapped[19] even now into my hand by an
     underskinker,[20] one that never spake other[21] English in his
     life than "Eight shillings and six pence," and "You are
     welcome," with this shrill addition, "Anon, anon, sir! Score[22]
25   a pint of bastard[23] in the Half Moon,"[24] or so.[25] But Ned, to
     drive[26] away the time till Falstaff come, I prithee do thou
     stand in some by-room,[27] while I question my puny[28] drawer
     to what end he gave me the sugar. And do thou never leave[29]
     calling "Francis!" that[30] his tale to me may be nothing but

12 drinking
13 work/boil/finish
14 have become
15 an apprentice, progressing learner
16 wandering utensil repairman (pots were usually made of "tin")
17 for the rest of
18 (small packets sold for sweetening sack)
19 slapped ("stuck")
20 assistant tapster/bartender (skink = to draw/pour liquor)
21 any other
22 make a record by drawing a mark/line★ (to ensure later payment: on the
   score = on account)
23 sweet Spanish wine
24 Half Moon = fancy name for a particular room in the inn
25 some such
26 pass
27 by-room = side/private room
28 (1) subordinate, assistant, (2) novice
29 leave off, stop
30 so that

"Anon!" Step aside and I'll show thee a precedent.[31] 30

POINS STEPS ASIDE

Poins (*within*) Francis!

Hal (*to Poins*) Thou art perfect. (*calling*) Francis!

ENTER DRAWER

Francis Anon, anon, sir. (*calling*) Look down into[32] the
Pomgarnet,[33] Ralph.

Hal Come hither, Francis. 35

Francis My lord.

Hal How long hast thou to serve,[34] Francis?

Francis Forsooth, five years, and as much as to –

Poins Francis!

Francis Anon, anon, sir. 40

Hal Five year! By'r lady,[35] a long lease[36] for the clinking of
pewter. But Francis, darest thou be so valiant as to play the
coward with thy indenture,[37] and show it a fair[38] pair of
heels, and run from it?

Francis O Lord sir, I'll be sworn[39] upon all the books in 45
England, I could find[40] in my heart –

Poins Francis!

---

31 what I have just been talking about (Quarto: present; Folio: president)
32 look down into = have a look at ("take care of")
33 pomegranate: another fancy name for an inn room
34 hast thou to serve = do you have to serve as an apprentice
35 by'r lady = by our Lady (Mary, Christ's mother)★
36 contract
37 contract★ (of apprenticeship)
38 fine, good
39 I'll be sworn = I would swear
40 find it

Francis Anon, sir.

Hal How old art thou, Francis?

50 *Francis* Let me see, about Michaelmas[41] next I shall be –

Poins Francis!

Francis (*calling*) Anon, sir. Pray stay a little, my lord.

Hal Nay, but hark you Francis, for the sugar thou gavest me, 'twas a pennyworth, was't not?

55 *Francis* O Lord, I would it had been two.

Hal I will give thee for it a thousand pound. Ask me when thou wilt, and thou shalt have it.

Poins Francis!

Francis Anon, anon.

60 *Hal* Anon, Francis? No, Francis, but tomorrow, Francis – or Francis, a[42] Thursday – or indeed, Francis, when thou wilt. But Francis.

Francis My lord.

Hal Wilt thou rob this[43] leathern-jerkin, crystal-button, not-
65 pated,[44] agate-ring, puke-stocking,[45] caddis[46]-garter, smooth-tongue, Spanish[47] pouch?[48]

Francis O Lord sir, who do you mean?

Hal Why then your brown bastard[49] is your only drink.[50]

41 29 September (MIkilMUS)
42 on
43 the description fits an innkeeper; "rob" refers back to the apprentice indenture with the innkeeper
44 close-cropped, short-haired
45 woolen cloth of a darkish color
46 crewel, worsted
47 Spanish-leather
48 an outside pocket/bag
49 sweet Spanish wine (like muscatel)
50 your only drink = the only drink for you

For look you, Francis, your white canvas doublet[51] will
sully.[52] In Barbary,[53] sir, it cannot come to so much.[54]   70

Francis What sir?

Poins Francis!

Hal Away, you rogue, dost thou not hear them call.

THEY BOTH CALL HIM. THE DRAWER STANDS STUPEFIED,
NOT KNOWING WHICH WAY TO GO

ENTER VINTNER[55]

Vintner What? Stand'st thou still and hear'st such a calling? Look
to the guests[56] within. (*to Hal*) My lord, old Sir John with half   75
a dozen more are at the door. Shall I let them in?

Hal Let them alone[57] awhile, and then open the door.

EXIT VINTNER

(*calling*) Poins.

Poins (*still within*) Anon, anon, sir.

ENTER POINS

Hal Sirrah, Falstaff and the rest of the thieves are at the door.   80
Shall we be merry?

Poins As merry as crickets,[58] my lad. But hark ye, what

51 close-fitting body garment worn by both sexes (with or without sleeves)
52 stain
53 Barbary sugar
54 (more or less doubletalk, clearly intended to confuse Francis)
55 wine seller, innkeeper
56 customers, patrons
57 let them alone = leave them alone, let them wait
58 (proverbial: crickets are always "singing")

cunning match[59] have you made with this jest of the drawer?
Come, what's the issue?[60]

85. *Hal*   I am now of all humors that have showed themselves[61]
humors since the old days of good man Adam, to the pupil[62]
age of this present twelve o'clock at midnight. (*to Francis*)
What's o'clock, Francis?

Francis Anon, anon, sir.

90. *Hal*   That ever this fellow should have fewer words than a
parrot, and yet[63] the son of a woman! His industry[64] is up
stairs and down stairs, his eloquence the parcel[65] of a
reckoning.[66] I am not yet of Percy's mind,[67] the Hotspur of
the North, he that kills me[68] some six or seven dozen of Scots

95. at a breakfast, washes his hands, and says to his wife, "Fie upon
this quiet life, I want[69] work." "O my sweet Harry," says she,
"how many hast thou killed today?" "Give my roan horse a
drench,"[70] says he, and answers, "Some fourteen," an hour
after. "A trifle, a trifle."

100.   I prithee call in Falstaff. I'll play Percy, and that damned
brawn[71] shall play Dame Mortimer his wife. "Rivo!"[72] says

---

59 cunning match = clever/witty/sly★ contest/game
60 result, conclusion
61 showed themselves = showed themselves to be
62 infant
63 yet be
64 (1) skill, intelligence, (2) effort, exertion
65 dividing up, apportioning, sharing★
66 bill
67 judgment, opinion, disposition
68 kills me = kills (hybrid form of the grammatical reflexive)
69 (1) need, (2) lack, (3) desire
70 drink
71 fat pig (Falstaff)
72 then a common exclamation at drinking bouts/parties

the drunkard. Call in Ribs,[73] call in Tallow.[74]

ENTER FALSTAFF

Poins   Welcome Jack, where hast thou been?

Falstaff A plague of[75] all cowards, I say, and a[76] vengeance too,
marry and amen! Give me a cup of sack, boy. Ere I lead this   105
life long, I'll sew nether-stocks,[77] and mend them, and foot[78]
them too. A plague of all cowards. Give me a cup of sack,
rogue, is there no virtue extant?[79]

HE DRINKS

Hal   Didst thou never see Titan[80] kiss[81] a dish of butter
(pitiful-hearted[82] Titan) that[83] melted at the sweet tale[84] of   110
the sun?[85] If thou didst, then behold that compound.[86]

Falstaff You rogue, here's lime[87] in this sack too. There is
nothing but roguery to be found in villainous man, yet a

---

73 ox meat, pork meat
74 suet, animal fat (rendered off by boiling)
75 on
76 with a
77 stockings (upper-stock = upper/wider hose; nether-stock = lower/*
   narrower hose)
78 make/add/attach a foot to a stocking
79 virtue extant = morality/diligence existing/left alive
80 (?) sun god (Falstaff's florid face, poised over the cup of wine, and causing it
   to "melt" away)
81 press its rays down on
82 pitiful-hearted = tender-hearted (the sun's tenderness softens/melts the
   butter)
83 the butter
84 (?) sweet tale = pleasing presence/weight (as in "by tale/by measure": see
   OED, tale, 2.6.b)
85 Folio: sun; Quarto: sun's
86 mixture
87 added to clarify the wine

coward is worse than a cup of sack with lime in it. A
115 villainous coward. Go thy ways,[88] old Jack, die when thou
wilt. If manhood, good manhood be[89] not forgot upon the
face of the earth, then am I a shotten[90] herring. There lives
not three good men unhanged in England, and one of them is
fat, and grows old, God help the while. A bad world, I say. I
120 would I were a weaver, I could sing psalms,[91] or anything.
A plague of all cowards, I say still.

Hal   How now, wool-sack,[92] what mutter you?

Falstaff A king's son? If I do not beat thee out of thy kingdom
with a dagger of lath,[93] and drive all thy subjects afore thee
125 like a flock of wild geese, I'll never wear hair on my face
more.[94] You Prince of Wales?

Hal   Why, you whoreson round-man, what's the matter?

Falstaff Are not you a coward? Answer me to that, and[95] Poins
there.

130 *Poins*   Zounds, ye fat paunch, and[96] ye call me coward, by the
Lord I'll stab thee.

Falstaff I call thee coward? I'll see thee damned ere I call thee
coward. But I would give a thousand pound I could run as
fast as thou canst. You are straight[97] enough in the shoulders,

88 paths, roads
89 is
90 lean and thin, after having spawned
91 many weavers were Puritans
92 large package / bale of wool
93 narrow strip of wood (in the old morality plays, Vice★ would rage about,
brandishing – and sometimes striking with – a lath weapon)
94 any more
95 as well as
96 if
97 (1) erect, not crooked, (2) reliable, direct, honest

you care not who sees your back. Call you that backing of   135
your friends? A plague upon such backing, give me them that
will face me. Give me a cup of sack. I am a rogue if I drunk[98]
today.

Hal   O villain, thy lips are scarce wiped since thou drunk'st
last.   140

Falstaff All is one[99] for that. (*he drinks*) A plague of all cowards,
still say I.

Hal   What's the matter?

Falstaff What's the matter? There be four of us here have ta'en a
thousand pound this day morning.[100]   145

Hal   Where is it, Jack? Where is it?

Falstaff Where is it? Taken from us, it is. A hundred upon poor
four of us.

Hal   What, a hundred, man?

Falstaff I am a rogue if I were not at half-sword[101] with a dozen   150
of them two hours together.[102] I have scaped by miracle. I am
eight times thrust through the doublet, four through the
hose, my buckler cut through and through, my sword hacked
like[103] a handsaw – *ecce signum!*[104] (*exhibits his sword*) I never
dealt[105] better since I was a man. All would not do.[106] A   155
plague of all cowards! Let them speak. If they speak more or
less than truth, they are villains, and the sons of darkness.

---

 98 if I drunk = if I have drunk at all
 99 all is one = it's all the same
100 this day morning = this morning ("this day in the morning")
101 half-sword = close quarters
102 all together
103 as if by
104 behold the evidence
105 delivered blows
106 all would not do = all that was not enough

Hal   Speak sirs, how was it?

Gadshill We four set upon some dozen.

160 *Falstaff* Sixteen at least, my lord.

Gadshill And bound them.

Peto   No, no, they were not bound.

Falstaff You rogue, they were bound, every man of them, or I
am a Jew else, an 'Ebrew Jew.

165 *Gadshill* As we were sharing, some six or seven fresh[107] men set
upon us.

Falstaff And unbound the rest, and then come in the other.[108]

Hal   What, fought you with them all?

Falstaff All? I know not what you call all, but if I fought not

170 with fifty of them I am a bunch of radish.[109] If there were not
two or three and fifty upon poor old Jack, then am I no two-
legged creature.

Hal   Pray God you have not murdered some of them.

Falstaff Nay, that's past praying for,[110] I have peppered[111] two

175 of them. Two I am sure I have paid,[112] two rogues in buckram
suits.[113] I tell thee what, Hal, if I tell thee a lie, spit in my face,
call me horse. Thou knowest my old ward:[114] here I lay,[115]
and thus I bore my point. Four rogues in buckram let drive[116]
at me.

107 new
108 others
109 i.e., lean
110 past praying for = too late to be praying about
111 ruined, destroyed, killed★
112 paid back, satisfied (used ironically and meaning "killed")★
113 clothing
114 parrying move, in fencing (Folio: word)
115 was placed ("was")
116 let drive = struck

Hal	What, four? Thou saidst but two even now.	180
Falstaff	Four, Hal, I told thee four.	
Poins	Ay, ay, he said four.	
Falstaff	These four came all a-front,[117] and mainly[118] thrust at me. I made me no more ado, but took all their seven points in my target[119] – thus.	185
Hal	Seven? Why there were but four even now.	
Falstaff	In buckram.	
Poins	Ay, four in buckram suits.	
Falstaff	Seven, by these hilts,[120] or I am a villain else.	
Hal	Prithee let him alone, we shall have more[121] anon.	190
Falstaff	Dost thou hear me, Hal?	
Hal	Ay, and mark[122] thee too, Jack.	
Falstaff	Do so, for it is worth the list'ning to. These nine in buckram that I told thee of –	
Hal	So, two more already.	195
Falstaff	Their points[123] being broken –	
Poins	Down fell their hose.	
Falstaff	Began to give me ground. But I followed me close, came in,[124] foot and hand and, with[125] a thought, seven of the eleven I paid.	200

117 face to face, in direct opposition
118 mightily, violently
119 shield, buckler
120 by these hilts = I swear by this sword (hilt = handle: "formerly often in plural, with same sense," *OED*, hilt 1b, citing this usage in Shakespeare's *Henry V*)
121 i.e., it will soon be more than seven
122 (1) pay attention to, (2) take note of, (3) recognize
123 (1) sword points (as Falstaff intends), (2) garter laces (as Poins puns upon)
124 came in = got in under their guard
125 like, as fast as

Hal   O monstrous! Eleven buckram men grown out of two?

Falstaff   But as the Divel would have it, three misbegotten
knaves in Kendal green[126] came at my back, and let drive at
me. For it was so dark, Hal, that thou could'st not see thy
205   hand.

Hal   These lies are like their father that begets them,
gross[127] as a mountain, open,[128] palpable.[129] Why thou clay-
brained[130] guts, thou knotty-pated[131] fool, thou whoreson
obscene greasy tallow-catch[132] –

210 *Falstaff*   What, art thou mad? Art thou mad? Is not the truth the
truth?

Hal   Why, how couldst thou know[133] these men in Kendal
green when it was so dark thou could'st not see thy hand.
Come, tell us your reason.[134] What sayest thou to this?

215 *Poins*   Come, your reason, Jack, your reason.

Falstaff   What, upon compulsion?[135] Zounds, and[136] I were at
the strappado,[137] or all the racks[138] in the world, I would not
tell you on compulsion. Give you a reason on compulsion? If
reasons were as plentiful as blackberries, I would give no man

126 coarse, inexpensive wool
127 massive
128 bare, exposed, brazen
129 readily perceived
130 clay-brained = clod-headed, dull, stupid
131 knotty-pated = blockheaded
132 (1) roll of fat, (2) pan into which drips the fat from roasting meat
133 perceive, identify, recognize
134 justification, explanation
135 upon compulsion = under coercion
136 if
137 torture device, victims being repeatedly hung and let halfway down with a
     violent jerk
138 torture device, victims being pulled in two opposing directions

a reason upon compulsion, I.[139]   220

Hal   I'll be no longer guilty of this sin. This sanguine[140]
coward, this bed-presser,[141] this horse-back-breaker, this
huge hill of flesh –

Falstaff 'Sblood, you starveling,[142] you elf-skin,[143] you dried
neats-tongue,[144] you bull's-pizzle,[145] you stockfish[146] . . . O   225
for breath to utter what is like thee! You tailor's yard,[147] you
sheath, you bowcase,[148] you vile standing tuck.[149]

Hal   Well, breathe a while, and then to it again, and when
thou hast tired thyself in base comparisons hear me speak but
this.   230

Poins   Mark, Jack.

Hal   We two saw you four set on four, and bound them and
were masters[150] of their wealth. Mark now how a plain tale
shall put you down.[151] Then did we two set on you four, and
with a word outfaced[152] you from your prize, and have it, yea   235
and can show it you here in the house.[153] And Falstaff, you
carried your guts away as nimbly, with as quick dexterity,[154]

139 not I
140 sanguinary, bloody-minded
141 bed-bound fellow
142 emaciated
143 shriveled, shrunken
144 neat's-tongue = ox-tongue (food)
145 bull's-pizzle = bull's penis
146 codfish split open and cured hard by drying
147 yardstick
148 case for an archer's bow
149 standing tuck = inflexible/stiff rapier/straight sword
150 owners, in control★
151 put you down = crush/degrade/shame/refute you
152 forced
153 inn-house
154 readiness

and roared for mercy, and still run and roared, as ever I heard
bull-calf. What a slave[155] art thou to hack thy sword as thou
240   hast done, and then say it was in fight. What trick, what
device,[156] what starting hole[157] canst thou now find out, to
hide thee from this open and apparent shame?

Poins   Come, let's hear, Jack, what trick hast thou now?

Falstaff   By the Lord, I knew ye as well as he that made ye. Why
245   hear you, my masters, was it for me to kill the heir apparent?
Should I turn upon the true prince? Why, thou knowest I am
as valiant as Hercules. But beware instinct, the lion will not
touch the true prince, instinct is a great matter. I was now a
coward on instinct. I shall think the better of myself, and thee,
250   during my life, I for[158] a valiant lion, and thou for a true
prince. But by the Lord, lads, I am glad you have the money.
Hostess, clap to the doors![159] Watch tonight, pray tomorrow!
Gallants, lads, boys, hearts of gold, all the titles[160] of good
fellowship come to you! What, shall we be merry, shall we
255   have a play extempore?[161]

Hal   Content,[162] and the argument[163] shall be thy running
away.

Falstaff   Ah, no more of that, Hal, and[164] thou lovest me.

155 knave, rascal★
156 scheme, invention, ingenuity★
157 starting hole = loophole, refuge
158 for being
159 clap to the doors = slam the doors shut
160 names, descriptions
161 without preparation, improvised
162 yes, sure
163 theme, subject
164 if

ENTER HOSTESS

Hostess O Jesu,[165] my lord the Prince!

Hal How now, my lady the hostess, what say'st thou to me? 260

Hostess Marry my lord, there is a nobleman of the court at door
would speak with you. He says he comes from your father.

Hal Give him as much as will make him a royal man,[166] and
send him back again to my mother.

Falstaff What manner of man is he? 265

Hostess An old man.

Falstaff What doth Gravity[167] out of his bed at midnight? Shall
I give him his answer?

Hal Prithee do, Jack.

Falstaff 'Faith, and I'll send him packing.[168] 270

EXIT FALSTAFF

Hal Now sirs, by'r lady you fought fair.[169] So did you, Peto.
So did you, Bardolph. You are lions too, you ran away upon
instinct. You will not touch the true prince. No, fie!

Bardolph 'Faith, I ran when I saw others run.

Hal 'Faith, tell me now in earnest, how came Falstaff's 275
sword so hacked?

Peto Why, he hacked it with his dagger, and said he would
swear truth out of England,[170] but he would make you

165 Jesus
166 noble = a gold coin worth about 6 shillings; royal = a gold coin worth
about 10 shillings
167 what doth Gravity = what is Mister Solemnity/Authority/Dignity doing
168 send him packing = dismiss him
169 with honor/equity
170 swear truth out of England = swear in such high/exaggerated terms that
truth would flee the country

believe it was done in fight, and persuaded us to do the like.

280 *Bardolph*   Yea, and to tickle[171] our noses with speargrass,[172] to make them bleed, and then to beslubber[173] our garments with it,[174] and swear it was the blood of true men. I did that I did not[175] this seven year before, I blushed to hear his monstrous devices.

285 *Hal*   O villain, thou stolest a cup of sack eighteen years ago, and wert taken with[176] the manner,[177] and ever since thou hast blushed extempore. Thou hadst fire[178] and sword on thy side, and yet thou ran'st away. What instinct hadst thou for it?

Bardolph   My lord do you see these meteors?[179] (*pointing to his*
290   *face*) Do you behold these exhalations?[180]

Hal   I do.

Bardolph   What think you they portend?[181]

Hal   Hot livers,[182] and cold purses.[183]

Bardolph   Choler, my Lord, if rightly taken.[184]

ENTER FALSTAFF

295 *Hal*   No, if rightly taken, halter.[185] Here comes lean Jack,

171 poke
172 sharp-leafed weed
173 smear
174 the blood
175 that I did not = what I had not done
176 taken with = liked
177 usage, custom
178 firearms, guns
179 red pimples/boils
180 burning, fiery emanations
181 indicate, mean
182 hot livers = passionate/active livers (productive of much bile/spleen)
183 cold purses = chilled/empty purses
184 understood
185 rightly taken, halter = correctly/legally captured/arrested, hanged (halter = rope with a noose)*

here comes bare-bone. How now, my sweet creature of
bombast,[186] how long is't ago,[187] Jack, since thou sawest
thine own knee?

Falstaff   My own knee? When I was about thy years, Hal. I was
not an eagle's talon[188] in the waist, I could have crept into any   300
alderman's thumb-ring.[189] A plague of sighing and grief, it
blows a man up like a bladder.[190] There's villainous news
abroad. Here was Sir John Bracy, from your father. You must
to the court in the morning. That same mad fellow of the
north, Percy, and he of Wales that gave Amamon[191] the   305
bastinado,[192] and made Lucifer cuckold, and swore[193] the
Divel his true liegeman[194] upon the cross of a Welsh hook.[195]
What a plague call you him?[196]

Poins   O, Glendower.

Falstaff   Owen, Owen, the same, and his son-in-law Mortimer,   310
and old Northumberland, and that sprightly[197] Scot of Scots,
Douglas, that runs a-horseback up a hill perpendicular.

Hal   He that rides at high speed, and with his pistol kills a
sparrow flying.

Falstaff   You have hit it.   315

Hal   So did he never[198] the sparrow.

---

186 (1) cotton-wool padding, (2) overinflated language
187 gone by, past
188 the thickness of an eagle's claw
189 large, costly ring with a seal
190 "bag"
191 a devil
192 beating/thrashing (especially on the soles of the feet)
193 swore in ("enlisted")
194 vassal, feudal subordinate/underling
195 billhook: a staff ending in a hook (i.e., a Welsh weapon that has no cross)
196 what a plague call you him? = what in the plague do you call him?
197 lively, brisk
198 never hit

Falstaff   Well, that rascal hath good mettle in him, he will not
run.

Hal   Why, what a rascal art thou then, to praise him so for
320   running?

Falstaff   A-horseback (ye cuckoo), but afoot he will not budge a
foot.

Hal   Yes, Jack, upon instinct.

Falstaff   I grant ye, upon instinct. Well, he is there too, and one
325   Mordake, and a thousand blue caps[199] more. Worcester is
stolen away tonight, thy father's beard is turned white with
the news, you may buy land now as cheap as stinking[200]
mackerel.

Hal   Why then, it is like[201] if there come a hot June, and this
330   civil buffeting hold, we shall buy[202] maidenheads as they buy
hob-nails,[203] by the hundreds.

Falstaff   By the mass, lad, thou sayest true, it is like we shall have
good trading[204] that way. But tell me, Hal, art not thou
horrible afeard? Thou being heir apparent, could the world
335   pick thee out three such enemies again,[205] as that fiend
Douglas, that spirit Percy, and that divel Glendower? Art thou
not horribly afraid? Doth not thy blood thrill[206] at it?

---

199 blue caps = Scotsmen (in blue bonnets/hats)
200 spoiled, rotten
201 likely
202 obtain, take possession of ("why then" referring back to selling off
     unsellable goods: because of the coming war, "maidenheads" too can
     become unsalable and go at very cheap prices)
203 boot/shoe nails (short with large heads)
204 commerce, business
205 a second time
206 move fast(er)

Hal   Not a whit,[207] i'faith. I lack some of thy instinct.

Falstaff   Well, thou wilt be horribly chid[208] tomorrow, when
        thou comest to thy father. If thou love me, practice an answer.   340

Hal   Do thou stand for my father and examine[209] me upon
        the particulars[210] of my life.

Falstaff   Shall I? Content. This chair shall be my state,[211] this
        dagger my scepter,[212] and this cushion my crown.

Hal   Thy state is taken[213] for a joined stool,[214] thy golden   345
        scepter for a leaden dagger, and thy precious rich crown for a
        pitiful bald crown.[215]

Falstaff   Well, and[216] the fire of grace be not quite out of thee,
        now shalt thou be moved. Give me a cup of sack to make my
        eyes look red, that it may be thought I have wept, for I must   350
        speak in passion, and I will do it in King Cambyses' vein.[217]

Hal   Well, here is my leg.[218]

Falstaff   And here is my speech. Stand aside, nobility.[219]

Hostess   O Jesu, this is excellent sport, i'faith.

---

207 least little bit★
208 scolded, rebuked
209 test, question
210 details
211 chair of state, throne
212 rod-shaped, ornate symbol of kingly authority★
213 (1) assumed/undertaken/adopted, (2) gained, obtained, accepted, (3)
    pretended/affected
214 joined stool = stool made by a carpenter ("joiner") rather than by an
    unskilled workman
215 i.e., Falstaff's head
216 if
217 King Cambyses' vein = high-rhetorical rant much used in drama of the
    time
218 bow
219 i.e., everyone in his audience of inn-house denizens

355 *Falstaff* *(to Hostess)* Weep not, sweet queen,[220] for trickling[221]
tears are vain.

Hostess O the Father, how he holds his countenance![222]

Falstaff For God's sake, lords, convey[223] my tristful[224] queen,
For tears do stop[225] the floodgates of her eyes.

360 *Hostess* O Jesu, he doth it as like one of these harlotry[226] players
as ever I see.

Falstaff Peace, good pint-pot, peace, good tickle-brain.[227]

Harry, I marvel where thou spendest thy time, but also how
thou art accompanied.[228] For though the camomile[229] the

365 more it is trodden on, the faster it grows, so youth, the more it
is wasted, the sooner it wears.[230] That thou art my son I have
partly thy mother's word, partly my own opinion, but chiefly
a villainous trick[231] of thine eye, and a foolish hanging of thy
nether lip, that doth warrant[232] me. If then thou be son to

370 me, here lies the point. Why, being son to me, art thou so
pointed at?[233] Shall the blessèd sun of heaven prove a
micher,[234] and eat blackberries?[235] A question not to be

---

220 (1) queen of England, (2) whore, prostitute
221 flowing
222 bearing, comportment, demeanor, appearance*
223 lead/conduct away
224 sad
225 fill
226 scurvy, trashy
227 tickle-brain = potent liquor
228 in comradeship, with whom you are associating
229 aromatic creeping herb, bearing white flowers used medicinally
230 is destroyed/worn out
231 (1) habit, custom, (2) characteristic appearance
232 guarantee the matter for
233 pointed at = pointed at in scorn
234 secret/petty thief
235 eat blackberries: as truant schoolboys frequently and notoriously did

asked. Shall the son of England[236] prove a thief, and take
purses? A question to be asked. There is a thing, Harry, which
thou hast often heard of, and it is known to many in our land   375
by the name of pitch.[237] This pitch (as ancient writers do
report) doth defile, so doth the company thou keepest. For
Harry, now I do not speak to thee in drink, but in tears. Not
in pleasure, but in passion. Not in words only, but in woes
also. And yet there is a virtuous man, whom I have often   380
noted in thy company, but I know not his name.

Hal   What manner of man, and it like[238] your Majesty?

Falstaff A goodly portly[239] man, i'faith, and a corpulent. Of a
cheerful look, a pleasing eye, and a most noble carriage, and as
I think his age some fifty, or by'r Lady inclining[240] to   385
threescore. And now I remember me, his name is Falstaff. If
that man should be lewdly given,[241] he deceiveth me, for
Harry, I see virtue in his looks. If then the tree may be known
by the fruit, as the fruit by the tree, then peremptorily[242] I
speak it, there is virtue in that Falstaff. Him keep with, the   390
rest banish. And tell me now, thou naughty varlet, tell me
where hast thou been this month?

Hal   Dost thou speak like a king? Do thou stand for me, and
I'll play my father.

Falstaff Depose me.[243] If thou dost it half so gravely, so   395

---

236 the King
237 tar
238 and it like = if it please
239 (1) large, (2) dignified, stately
240 approaching, tending toward
241 should be lewdly given = were to be evilly/wickedly★ disposed
242 definitely, conclusively
243 depose me = deprive me of my office/authority

majestically, both in word and matter, hang me up by the
heels for a rabbit sucker,[244] or a poulter's[245] hare.

Hal (*sitting in the chair of state*) Well, here I am set.

Falstaff And here I stand. (*to the others*) Judge, my masters.

400 *Hal* Now Harry, whence come you?

Falstaff My noble lord, from Eastcheap.

Hal The complaints I hear of thee are grievous.[246]

Falstaff 'Sblood my lord, they are false. Nay, I'll tickle[247] ye
for[248] a young prince, i'faith.

405 *Hal* Swearest thou, ungracious[249] boy? Henceforth ne'er
look on me. Thou art violently carried away from grace.
There is a divel haunts thee, in the likeness of an old fat man:
a tun[250] of man is thy companion. Why do'st thou
converse[251] with that trunk[252] of humors,[253] that bolting-

410 hutch[254] of beastliness, that swollen parcel[255] of dropsies,[256]
that huge bombard[257] of sack, that stuffed cloak-bag[258] of
guts, that roasted Manningtree[259] ox with the pudding[260] in

244 baby
245 someone who sells poultry
246 oppressive, serious*
247 thrill, entertain, please
248 as, in the role of
249 (1) graceless, wicked, (2) rude, bad-mannered
250 large cask/barrel
251 associate, keep company
252 chest, coffer, box
253 morbid vapors
254 bolting-hutch = wasted chest/coffer/box
255 quantity, package
256 disease of water retention, swelling the body
257 jug, bottle
258 cloak-bag = valise, portmanteau
259 in East Anglia, site of annual fairs where famously large oxen were roasted
260 (1) meat pudding, sausage, (2) stuffing

his belly, that reverend Vice,[261] that gray iniquity,[262] that
father ruffian, that vanity in years?[263] Wherein is he good, but
to taste sack and drink it? Wherein neat and cleanly,[264] but to   415
carve a capon and eat it? Wherein cunning, but in craft?[265]
Wherein crafty,[266] but in villainy? Wherein villainous, but in
all things? Wherein worthy,[267] but in nothing?

Falstaff I would[268] your grace would take me with you.[269]
Whom means your grace?   420

Hal   That villainous abominable misleader of youth, Falstaff,
that old white-bearded Satan.

Falstaff My lord, the man I know.

Hal   I know thou do'st.

Falstaff But to say I know more harm in him than in myself,   425
were[270] to say more than I know. That he is old (the more the
pity), his white hairs do witness it, but that he is (saving your
reverence) a whoremaster, that I utterly deny. If sack and sugar
be a fault, God help the wicked. If to be old and merry be a
sin, then many an old host[271] that I know is damned. If to be   430
fat be[272] to be hated, then Pharaoh's lean kine[273] are to be

---

261 comic character in the old morality plays
262 unrighteousness
263 in years = old, agèd
264 neat and cleanly = shining/elegant/refined and clever/adroit/able
265 fraud, deceit
266 ingenious, skillful
267 excellent, valuable, distinguished★
268 wish
269 take me with you = help me to understand you
270 would be
271 innkeeper
272 is
273 in Pharaoh's dream, Genesis 41:17–21, "the lean and the ill favored kine did
     eat up the . . . seven fat kine" (kine = cattle)

loved. No, my good lord, banish Peto, banish Bardolph, banish
Poins, but for sweet Jack Falstaff, kind Jack Falstaff, true Jack
Falstaff, valiant Jack Falstaff – and therefore more valiant
435   being as he is old Jack Falstaff – banish not him thy Harry's
company, banish not him thy Harry's company. Banish plump
Jack, and banish all the world.

Hal   I do, I will.

ENTER BARDOLPH, RUNNING

Bardolph O my lord, my lord, the sheriff with a most monstrous
440   watch[274] is at the door.

Falstaff   Out[275] ye rogue, play out the play! I have much to say
in the behalf of that Falstaff.

ENTER HOSTESS

Hostess   O Jesu, my lord, my lord!

Hal   Heigh, heigh, the Devil rides upon a fiddle stick.[276]
445   What's the matter?

Hostess   The sheriff and all the watch are at the door. They are
come to search the house, shall I let them in?

Falstaff   Dost thou hear, Hal? Never[277] call a true piece of gold
a counterfeit.[278] Thou art essentially[279] made without
450   seeming so.[280]

---

274 most monstrous watch = huge / immense band of watchmen / constables
     (early form of police)
275 (1) go away, (2) damn you
276 the Devil rides upon a fiddle stick = much ado about nothing, what's the
     fuss all about (proverbial)
277 one should never (i.e., Hal is "true gold," though people – and his father –
     say he is not)
278 a counterfeit = spurious, not genuine
279 eminently, loftily ("royally")
280 essentially made without seeming so = you may not seem royal, but that's
     what you are (i.e., Hal is both royal and loyal)

Hal   And thou a natural coward without instinct.

Falstaff I deny your major.[281] If you will deny[282] the sheriff, so.[283] If not, let him enter. If I become not[284] a cart[285] as well as another man, a plague on my bringing up.[286] I hope I shall as soon[287] be strangled with a halter as another.   455

Hal   Go hide thee behind the arras.[288] The rest[289] walk up above.[290] Now my masters, for a true face, and good conscience.

Falstaff Both which I have had, but their date[291] is out,[292] and therefore I'll hide me.   460

EXEUNT ALL BUT HAL AND PETO

Hal   Call in the sheriff.

ENTER SHERIFF AND A CARRIER[293]

Hal   Now, master[294] sheriff, what is your will with me?

Sheriff First pardon me, my lord. A hue and cry[295]

281 (1) major premise (in syllogistic logic), (2) mayor (both Quarto and Folio spell the word "maior")
282 will deny = wish to refuse to admit (as one also refuses to admit a major premise)
283 do so, all right
284 become not = do not grace/adorn/suit/befit
285 hangman's cart, bringing victims to the gallows
286 bringing up = rearing, breeding, education
287 quickly
288 tapestry/screen/heavy curtain (like that which Polonius hides behind, in *Hamlet*)
289 rest of you (thieves)
290 up above = upstairs
291 time, duration
292 extinct, elapsed, exhausted, finished ("outdated," a wording not then in use)
293 one of the two Carriers in act 2, scene 1
294 mister (used in speaking to/of a man not a gentleman and so not entitled to be addressed as "sir")
295 hue and cry = pursuit of criminal(s), instigated by a constable or by a person victimized (the Carrier)

Hath followed certain men unto this house.

465 *Hal*   What men?

Sheriff   One of them is well known, my gracious lord,

A gross fat man.

Carrier   As fat as butter.

Hal   The man I do assure you is not here,

For I myself at this time have employed him.[296]

470   And sheriff, I will engage[297] my word to thee,

That I will by tomorrow dinner time

Send him to answer[298] thee, or any man,

For any thing he shall be charged withal.

And so let me entreat[299] you leave the house.

475 *Sheriff*   I will, my lord. There are two gentlemen

Have in this robbery lost three hundred marks.

Hal   It may be so. If he have robbed these men,

He shall be answerable.[300] And so farewell.

Sheriff   Good night, my noble lord.

480 *Hal*   I think it is good morrow, is it not?

Sheriff   Indeed, my lord, I think it be two o'clock.

EXEUNT SHERIFF AND CARRIER

Hal   This oily rascal is known as well as Paul's.[301] Go call him
forth.

Peto   Falstaff! Fast asleep behind the arras, and snorting like a
485   horse.

---

296 employed him = given him something to do, sent him somewhere
297 pledge
298 respond to a legal charge
299 ask, request
300 ANseRAble
301 St. Paul's Cathedral, London

Hal Hark how hard he fetches breath. Search his pockets.

PETO SEARCHES AND FINDS PAPERS[302]

Hal What hast thou found?
Peto Nothing but papers, my lord.
Hal Let's see what they be.[303] Read them.

PETO READS

Item, a capon. Two shillings, two pence.[304]   490
Item, sauce. Four pence.
Item, sack, two gallons. Five shillings, eight pence.
Item, anchovies and sack, after supper. Two shillings, six
pence.
Item, bread. Ob.[305]   495
Hal O monstrous! But[306] one halfpennyworth of bread to[307]
this intolerable[308] deal of sack? What there is else, keep close,
we'll read it at more advantage.[309] There let him sleep till day.
I'll to the court[310] in the morning. We must all to[311] the
wars, and thy place[312] shall be honorable. I'll procure this fat   500
rogue a charge of foot,[313] and I know his death will be a

302 documents
303 Folio: be they
304 pennies
305 obolus, halfpenny
306 just
307 with, set against
308 (1) unbearable, insufferable, (2) extremely great, excessive
309 at more advantage = under better/more favorable circumstances
310 the King's court, *not* the law court
311 go to
312 position, post★
313 charge of foot = commission as commanding officer of a company of
   infantry/foot soldiers★

march[314] of twelve score.[315] The money shall be paid back again, with advantage.[316] Be with me betimes[317] in the morning. And so good morrow, Peto.

505 *Peto* Good morrow, good my lord.

EXEUNT

314 i.e., if he is obliged to make a march
315 240 (feet)
316 an increase in the sum
317 very early

Act 3

SCENE I

Wales. Glendower's castle

ENTER HOTSPUR, WORCESTER, MORTIMER, GLENDOWER

Mortimer   These promises are fair,[1] the parties sure,[2]
And our induction[3] full of prosperous[4] hope.

Hotspur   Lord Mortimer, and cousin Glendower, will you[5] sit
down?
And uncle Worcester. A plague upon it,
I have forgot the map.

Glendower   No, here it is.   5
Sit, cousin Percy, sit good cousin Hotspur.
For by that name as oft as Lancaster[6]
Doth speak of you, his cheek looks pale, and with

---

1 handsome, fine
2 safe, secure, not risky
3 introduction, initial step
4 thriving, propitious
5 will you = do you wish to
6 the King

A rising[7] sigh he wisheth you in heaven.

10 *Hotspur*   And you in hell,

As oft as he hears Owen Glendower spoke of.

Glendower I cannot blame him. At my nativity[8]

The front[9] of heaven was full of fiery shapes

Of burning cressets,[10] and at my birth

15 The frame and huge foundation of the earth

Shaked like a coward.

Hotspur   Why so it would have done

At the same season[11] if your mother's cat

Had but kittened, though yourself had never been born.

Glendower I say the earth did shake when I was born.

20 *Hotspur*   And I say the earth was not of my mind,

If you suppose as[12] fearing you it shook.

Glendower The heavens were all on fire, the earth did tremble.

Hotspur   O then the earth shook to see the heavens on fire,

And not in fear of your nativity.

25 Diseasèd nature oftentimes breaks forth

In strange eruptions. Oft the teeming[13] earth

Is with a kind of colic[14] pinched and vexed[15]

By the imprisoning of unruly[16] wind

Within her womb, which[17] for enlargement[18] striving

7 increasing, growing
8 birth
9 forehead, face
10 metal fire-baskets, burning grease or oil (used as beacons)
11 time, period
12 because
13 fertile, productive, sprouting
14 paroxysms / griping pains of the belly / bowels
15 pinched and vexed = squeezed and troubled / irritated / distressed
16 turbulent, disordered, ungovernable
17 which wind
18 (1) expansion, (2) release from confinement

Shakes the old beldam[19] earth, and topples down   30
Steeples and mossgrown towers. At your birth
Our grandam earth, having this distemp'rature,[20]
In passion shook.

Glendower   Cousin, of[21] many men
I do not bear these crossings.[22] Give me leave[23]
To tell you once again that at my birth   35
The front of heaven was full of fiery shapes,
The goats ran from the mountains, and the herds
Were strangely clamorous to[24] the frighted fields.
These signs have marked me extraordinary,[25]
And all the courses[26] of my life do show   40
I am not in the roll[27] of common men.
Where is he living, clipped[28] in with the sea
That chides[29] the banks of England, Scotland, Wales,
Which calls me pupil, or hath read[30] to me?
And[31] bring him out, that is but woman's son,   45
Can trace me[32] in the tedious ways of art,[33]
And hold me pace[34] in deep experiments.

19 grandmother
20 unwholesomeness, unhealthiness, disturbance
21 from
22 contradictions, thwarting*
23 give me leave = excuse me
24 clamorous to = crying/noisy in/on
25 EKstraORdiNAry
26 (1) paths, directions, proceedings, (2) stages
27 register, list, catalogue
28 hugged, embraced, surrounded, encircled
29 yelps/cries/drives at
30 taught/explained/lectured
31 and also
32 trace me = follow/stay with
33 learning, science
34 hold me pace = match/equal/keep up with me

Hotspur   I think there's no man speaks better Welsh.
    I'll to dinner.

50 *Mortimer*   Peace, cousin Percy, you will make him mad.[35]

Glendower   I can call spirits from the vasty deep.

Hotspur   Why so can I, or so can any man.
    But will they come when you do call for them?

Glendower   Why, I can teach you, cousin, to command the
    Devil.

55 *Hotspur*   And I can teach thee, coz, to shame the Devil,
    By telling truth. "Tell truth and shame the Devil."[36]
    If thou have power to raise him, bring him hither,
    And I'll be sworn I have power to shame him hence.
    O while you live tell truth and shame the Devil.

60 *Mortimer*   Come, come, no more of this unprofitable chat.[37]

Glendower   Three times hath Henry Bolingbroke[38] made head[39]
    Against my power,[40] thrice from the banks of Wye,[41]
    And sandy-bottomed Severn,[42] have I sent him
    Bootless home, and weather-beaten back.

65 *Hotspur*   Home without boots, and in foul weather too.
    How scapes he agues,[43] in the Devil's name?

Glendower   Come, here is the map. Shall we divide our right[44]

---

35 frenzied, wild, out of his mind
36 proverbial
37 come COME no MORE of THIS unPROfiTABle CHAT (iambic
    hexameter, rather than pentameter)
38 the King
39 made head = advanced
40 (1) strength, might, (2) army
41 river flowing from Wales into SW England
42 river flowing from central Wales into W England
43 fevers (EYgyuwz)
44 rights, claims, spheres, shares

According to our threefold order ta'en?

Mortimer The Archdeacon hath divided it

Into three limits very equally.   70

England from Trent, and Severn (*pointing*) hitherto,[45]

By[46] south and east is to my part assigned.

All westward, Wales beyond the Severn shore,

And all the fertile land within that bound

To Owen Glendower. (*to Hotspur*) And, dear coz, to you   75

The remnant northward, lying off[47] from Trent.

And our indentures tripartite are drawn,[48]

Which being sealed interchangeably[49]

(A business that this night may execute[50]),

Tomorrow, cousin Percy, you and I   80

And my good Lord of Worcester, will set forth

To meet your father and the Scottish power,

As is[51] appointed us at Shrewsbury.[52]

My father[53] Glendower is not ready yet,

Nor shall we need his help these fourteen days.   85

(*to Glendower*) Within that space[54] you may have drawn together

Your tenants, friends, and neighboring gentlemen.

45 up to here
46 and beyond
47 some distance offshore
48 written out in proper form
49 sealed interchangeably = each of three copies attested (using heated wax into which a seal has been impressed) reciprocally/mutually by all of the signing parties
50 carry out
51 was
52 city in W England
53 father-in-law (marital connections were not distinguished from birth ties)
54 time ("space of time")

Glendower A shorter time shall send me to you, lords,
And in my conduct[55] shall your ladies come,
90 From whom you now must steal and take no leave,
For there will be a world of water shed,
Upon the parting of your wives and you.
Hotspur   Methinks my moiety,[56] north from Burton here,
In quantity equals not one of yours.
95 See how this river comes me cranking[57] in,
And cuts me from the best of all my land
A huge half moon, a monstrous cantle[58] out.[59]
I'll have the current in this place dammed up,
And here the smug[60] and silver Trent shall run
100 In a new channel, fair and evenly.
It shall not wind with such a deep indent,
To rob me of so rich a bottom[61] here.
Glendower Not wind? It shall, it must, you see it doth.
Mortimer Yea,
105 But mark how he[62] bears his course, and runs me up
With like advantage on the other side,
Gelding[63] the opposèd continent[64] as much
As on the other side it takes from you.

55 escort
56 share, part
57 winding, crookedly
58 corner, nook, angle, slice
59 cuts me . . . out
60 smooth
61 low-lying land
62 it (the river)
63 cutting, depriving
64 opposèd continent = opposite mainland ("space/bulk/area")

Worcester   Yea, but[65] a little charge[66] will trench[67] him here,

    And on this north side win this cape[68] of land,   110

    And then he runs straight and even.

Hotspur   I'll have it so, a little charge will do it.

Glendower I'll not have it altered.

Hotspur   Will not you?

Glendower No, nor you shall not.[69]

Hotspur   Who shall say me nay?

Glendower Why that will I.   115

Hotspur   Let me not understand you then, speak it in Welsh.

Glendower I can speak English, lord, as well as you.

    For I was trained up[70] in the English court,

    Where being but young I framed to[71] the harp

    Many an English ditty[72] lovely[73] well,   120

    And gave the tongue[74] a helpful ornament –

    A virtue that was never seen in you.

Hotspur Marry, and I am glad of it with all my heart.

    I had rather be a kitten and cry mew,

    Than one of these same meter[75] ballad-mongers.[76]   125

65 just
66 expense
67 cut, divide, sever
68 projecting piece of land
69 nor you shall not = neither will you
70 educated
71 framed to = prepared/composed/adapted for
72 song
73 beautifully
74 English language
75 meter-measuring, metrical counting
76 ballad-mongers = ballad-makers/dealers

I had rather hear a brazen[77] canstick[78] turned,[79]

Or a dry wheel grate on the axle-tree,[80]

And that would set my teeth nothing[81] on edge,

Nothing so much as mincing[82] poetry.

130 'Tis like the forced[83] gait of a shuffling[84] nag.

Glendower Come, you shall have Trent turned.

Hotspur   I do not care. I'll give thrice so much land

To any well-deserving friend.

But in the way of bargain,[85] mark ye me,

135 I'll cavil[86] on the ninth part of a hair.

Are the indentures drawn? Shall we be gone?

Glendower The moon shines fair, you may away by night.[87]

I'll haste the writer.[88] And withal[89]

Break with[90] your wives of your departure hence.

140 I am afraid my daughter will run mad,

So much she doteth[91] on her Mortimer.

EXIT

Mortimer   Fie, cousin Percy, how you cross my father.

77 brass
78 candlestick
79 turned and cut on a lathe
80 axle-tree = in Shakespeare's time, the wooden pole on which carriage/cart
   wheels turned
81 would set . . . nothing = would not set
82 affectedly elegant/dainty
83 strained, stiff
84 hoof-dragging
85 bargaining
86 make fussy/unnecessary objections
87 away by night = leave by the end of the night
88 scribe, scrivener
89 in addition★
90 break with = make known/reveal/divulge to
91 is infatuated/foolishly in love with

Hotspur   I cannot choose. Sometime he angers me
    With telling me of the moldwarp[92] and the ant,
    Of the dreamer Merlin and his prophecies,   145
    And of a dragon, and a finless fish,
    A clip-winged griffin,[93] and a molten[94] raven,
    A couching[95] lion, and a ramping[96] cat,
    And such a deal of skimble-skamble stuff[97]
    As puts me from my faith.[98] I tell you what,   150
    He held me last night at least nine hours,
    In reckoning up the several[99] divels' names
    That were his lackies.[100] I cried "Hum," and "Well, go to,"[101]
    But marked him[102] not a word. O he is as tedious
    As a tired horse, a railing[103] wife,   155
    Worse than a smoky house. I had rather live
    With cheese and garlic in a windmill, far,[104]
    Than feed on cates[105] and have him talk to me
    In any summer house[106] in Christendom.
Mortimer   In faith he is a worthy gentleman,   160

---

92 mole
93 mythical animal with eagle's head and wings and lion's body and hind
    quarters
94 featherless ("molted")
95 crouching
96 rearing, with ferocity
97 rubbishy / nonsensical worthlessness
98 puts me from my faith = makes me cease to be a Christian (i.e., one who is
    forgiving)
99 separate, different, various
100 servile followers / servants
101 go to = come on (exclamation: "come off it")
102 (?) (1) he paid no attention to me, *or* (2) I paid no attention to him
103 abusive, quarrelsome
104 far rather
105 dainty / expensive food
106 summer house = cool, shady place

Exceedingly well read, and profited
In[107] strange concealments,[108] valiant as a lion,
And wondrous affable,[109] and as bountiful[110]
As mines of India. Shall I tell you, cousin?
165   He holds your temper[111] in a high respect
And curbs himself even of his natural scope,[112]
When you come cross his humor, faith he does.
I warrant you that man is not alive
Might so have tempted him as you have done,
170   Without the taste of danger and reproof.
But do not use it[113] oft, let me entreat you.
Worcester In faith my lord, you are too willful blame,[114]
And since your coming hither have done enough
To put him quite besides[115] his patience.
175   You must needs learn, lord, to amend this fault.
Though sometimes it shew[116] greatness, courage, blood[117]
(And that's the dearest grace it renders you),
Yet oftentimes it doth present harsh rage,
Defect[118] of manners, want[119] of government,
180   Pride, haughtiness, opinion,[120] and disdain,

107 profited in = one who has benefited from
108 secrets
109 courteous, civil
110 generous
111 character
112 intentions, disposition
113 use it = do this
114 willful blame = obstinately/perversely/strong-willedly to blame
115 out of
116 shows
117 lineage, descent
118 deFECT
119 lack
120 arrogance, dogmatism

The least of which, haunting[121] a nobleman,
Looseth men's hearts and leaves behind a stain
Upon the beauty of all parts besides,
Beguiling[122] them of commendation.[123]

Hotspur   Well, I am schooled.[124] Good manners be your
speed![125]   185
Here come our wives, and let us take our leave.

ENTER GLENDOWER WITH LADIES

Mortimer   This is the deadly spite[126] that angers me,
My wife can speak no English, I no Welsh.

Glendower My daughter weeps, she'll not part with you,
She'll be a soldier too, she'll to the wars.   190

Mortimer   Good father, tell her that she and my Aunt Percy
Shall follow in your conduct speedily.

GLENDOWER SPEAKS TO HER IN WELSH,
AND SHE ANSWERS HIM IN THAT LANGUAGE

Glendower She is desperate[127] here,
A peevish self-willed harlotry,[128] one
That no persuasion can do good upon.   195

THE LADY SPEAKS IN WELSH

Mortimer   I understand thy looks. That pretty Welsh[129]

121 habitually/frequently associated with
122 cheating
123 approval, reputation (KAminDEYseeOWN)
124 (1) taught, (2) disciplined
125 prosperity, good fortune
126 deadly spite = extreme annoyance/irritation
127 desperate here = despairing/hopeless staying here
128 loose/uncontrolled behavior (in Shakespeare's time, "harlot" was used to
      characterize both men and women)
129 i.e., her tears as "language"

Which thou pourest down from these swelling heavens[130]
I am too perfect[131] in, and but for shame
In such a parley[132] should I answer thee.[133]

SHE SPEAKS AGAIN IN WELSH

200 *Mortimer*   I understand thy kisses, and thou mine,
And that's a feeling disputation.[134]
But I will never be a truant,[135] love,
Till I have learned thy language, for thy tongue
Makes Welsh as sweet as ditties highly[136] penned,
205 Sung by a fair queen in a summer's bower,
With ravishing division,[137] to her lute.
Glendower   Nay, if you melt, then will she run mad.

SHE SPEAKS AGAIN IN WELSH

Mortimer   O, I am ignorance itself in this.
Glendower   She bids you on the wanton[138] rushes lay you down,
210 And rest your gentle head upon her lap,
And she will sing the song that pleaseth you,
And on your eyelids crown the god of sleep,
Charming your blood with pleasing heaviness,
Making such difference[139] 'twixt wake and sleep,
215 As is the difference betwixt[140] day and night,

130 swelling heavens = full to overflowing heavenly eyes
131 too perfect = only too accomplished
132 discourse ("use of language")
133 i.e., he would weep, too
134 feeling disputation = an emotional/sentient interchange of ideas/
      discourse/conversation (DISpuTAYseeOWN)
135 lazy/beggarly person
136 supremely, excellently, intensely
137 accompaniment
138 sportive, frisky
139 DIfeRENCE
140 DIfrence BeTWIXT (English was then a good deal more flexible)

The hour before the heavenly-harnessed team[141]
Begins his golden progress in the east.

Mortimer   With all my heart I'll sit and hear her sing.
By that time will our book[142] I think be drawn.

Glendower Do so,   220
And those musicians that shall play to you
Hang in the air a thousand leagues from hence,
And straight they shall be here. Sit and attend.

Hotspur   Come Kate, thou art perfect in lying down. Come
quick,
Quick, that I may lay my head in thy lap.   225

Kate   Go,[143] ye giddy[144] goose.

MUSIC

Hotspur   Now I perceive the Divel understands Welsh,
And 'tis no marvel he is so humorous.[145]
By'r Lady, he is a good musician.[146]

Kate   Then should[147] you be nothing but musical,   230
For you are altogether governed by humors.
Lie still, ye thief, and hear the lady sing in Welsh.

Hotspur   I had rather hear, lady, my brach[148] howl in Irish.

Kate   Wouldst thou have thy head broken?[149]

Hotspur   No.   235

Kate   Then be still.

141 i.e., the sun god's horses and chariot
142 document
143 go to (see Finding List)
144 mad, flighty, inconstant
145 capricious, fantastic, moody
146 muSIseeAN
147 must
148 bitch-hound
149 wounded, cracked

Hotspur Neither,[150] 'tis a woman's fault.

Kate Now God help thee!

Hotspur To the Welsh lady's bed.

240 *Kate* What's that?

Hotspur Peace, she sings.

THE LADY SINGS A WELSH SONG

Hotspur Come Kate, I'll have[151] your song too.

Kate Not mine, in good sooth.[152]

Hotspur Not yours, in good sooth? Heart,[153] you swear like a

245 comfit[154]-maker's wife. Not you, "in good sooth," and "as true

as I live," and "As God shall mend me," and "As sure as day."

And givest such sarcenet surety for[155] thy oaths,

As if thou never walkst further than Finsbury.[156]

Swear me, Kate, like a lady, as thou art,

250 A good mouth-filling oath, and leave "In sooth,"

And such protest[157] of[158] pepper ginger bread[159]

To velvet guards,[160] and Sunday citizens.[161]

150 once again, no
151 I'll have = I wish / want to have
152 truth
153 my heart
154 sweetmeat, candy
155 givest such sarcenet surety for = you offer / supply such a thin / flimsy
     pledge (sarcenet = fine / soft silk)
156 Finsbury Fields, N of Moorfields: resort near London, patronized by
     middle-class people, to whom Hotspur is determinedly hostile
157 declarations, rejections (proTEST)
158 of the nature of / like
159 i.e., pepper ginger bread lacked sufficient pepper to give it more than a
     passing tang
160 ornamental borders / trimming on clothing (frequently worn by
     shopkeepers)
161 Sunday citizens = bourgeois people

Come sing.

Kate   I will not sing.

Hotspur   'Tis[162] the next[163] way to turn tailor,[164] or be   255
      redbreast[165] teacher. And[166] the indentures be drawn, I'll
      away within these two hours. And so come in when ye will.

EXIT HOTSPUR

Glendower Come, come, Lord Mortimer, you are as slow
      As hot Lord Percy is on fire to go.
      By this[167] our book is drawn. We'll but seal,   260
      And then to horse immediately.

Mortimer   With all my heart.

EXEUNT

---

162 singing is
163 shortest
164 turn tailor = become a tailor (singing as they sewed)
165 be redbreast = be a singing
166 if
167 this time

SCENE 2

London, the palace

ENTER THE KING, HAL, AND OTHERS

King Lords, give us leave. The Prince of Wales and I
    Must have some private conference.[1] But be near at hand,
    For we shall presently have need of you.

EXEUNT LORDS

    I know not whether God will have it so
5   For some displeasing service I have done,
    That in his secret doom[2] out of[3] my blood
    He'll breed revengement[4] and a scourge for me.
    But thou dost in thy passages[5] of life
    Make me believe that thou art only marked[6]
10   For the hot vengeance, and the rod[7] of heaven,
    To punish my mistreadings.[8] Tell me else[9]
    Could such inordinate[10] and low desires,
    Such poor, such bare, such lewd, such mean attempts,
    Such barren pleasures, rude society
15   As thou art matched withal, and grafted[11] to,

1 CONfrence
2 (1) decree, judgment, (2) condemnation, punishment
3 out of = from
4 retribution, punishment, revenge
5 stages, pathways
6 distinguished, marked out
7 stick-like instrument of punishment
8 misdeeds
9 if otherwise
10 irregular, uncontrolled, excessive
11 joined

Accompany[12] the greatness of thy blood,
And hold their level[13] with thy princely heart?

Hal So please your Majesty, I would I could
Quit[14] all offenses with as clear excuse,
As well as I am doubtless[15] I can purge   20
Myself of many I am charged withal.
Yet such extenuation[16] let me beg
As in reproof[17] of many tales devised,
Which oft the ear of greatness needs must hear
By[18] smiling pickthanks,[19] and base newsmongers,   25
I may for some things true (wherein my youth
Hath faulty wandered and irregular),[20]
Find pardon on[21] my true submission.[22]

King God pardon thee. Yet let me wonder, Harry,
At thy affections,[23] which do hold a wing[24]   30
Quite from[25] the flight of all thy ancestors.
Thy place in council thou hast rudely lost,
Which by thy younger brother is supplied,
And art almost an alien to the hearts

12 consort/join with
13 hold their level = be on an equality
14 redeem, absolve, acquit
15 certain, sure
16 mitigation, lessening, modification
17 refutation, disproof
18 by means of, from
19 flatterers, sycophants
20 been disorderly/lawless ("wandered . . . faulty and irregular")
21 from, because of, based on
22 abasement, acceptance of correction
23 feelings, emotions, passions
24 hold a wing = fly, move
25 distant/different from

35 Of all the court and princes of my blood.

The hope and expectation of thy time

Is ruined, and the soul of every man

Prophetically do forethink[26] thy fall.

Had I so lavish[27] of my presence been,

40 So common hackneyed[28] in the eyes of men,

So stale[29] and cheap to vulgar[30] company,

Opinion,[31] that did help me to the Crown,

Had still kept[32] loyal to possession,[33]

And left me in reputeless[34] banishment,

45 A fellow of no mark nor likelihood.

By being seldom seen, I could not stir

But like a comet I was wondered at,

That[35] men would tell their children, "This is he."

Others would say, "Where, which is Bolingbroke?"

50 And then I stole all courtesy from heaven,[36]

And dressed myself in such humility

That I did pluck allegiance from men's hearts,

Loud shouts and salutations from their mouths,

Even in the presence of the crownèd king.

55 Thus did I keep my person[37] fresh and new,

26 anticipate
27 unrestrained, wild, wasteful
28 common hackneyed = publicly indiscriminate
29 worn out, past its prime
30 to vulgar = in/with ordinary/lower-class
31 general belief, reputation*
32 stayed
33 occupancy, ownership (i.e., to the reigning king, Richard II: poSEsiON)
34 inglorious, without reputation
35 so that
36 all courtesy from heaven = all of heaven's courtesy
37 character, personage

My presence like a robe pontifical,[38]
Ne'er seen but wondered at. And so my state,[39]
Seldom[40] but sumptuous, showed like a feast,
And won by rareness such[41] solemnity.
The skipping[42] king,[43] he ambled[44] up and down,   60
With shallow jesters, and rash bavin[45] wits,
Soon kindled and soon burned, carded his state,[46]
Mingled his royalty with cap'ring[47] fools,
Had his great name profanèd[48] with their scorns,[49]
And gave his countenance against his name[50]   65
To laugh at[51] gibing boys, and stand the push[52]
Of every beardless vain comparative,[53]
Grew a companion[54] to the common[55] streets,
Enfeoffed[56] himself to popularity,
That being daily swallowed by men's eyes,   70

38 bishop-/pope-like
39 condition, welfare★
40 infrequent ("scarce")
41 i.e., so much
42 i.e., jumping about, as in children's skipping
43 Richard II
44 gliding smoothly/evenly/easily
45 rash bavin = reckless/impetuous easily inflammable
46 carded his state = adulterated his majesty
47 dancing
48 blasphemed, desecrated
49 their scorns = the contempt/mockery (1) felt *for* fools, or (2) felt *by* fools
50 (1) rank, title, (2) reputation
51 laugh at = be laughed at by
52 blows, knocks
53 humorist
54 associate, sharer
55 (1) public, (2) ordinary (negative)★
56 surrendered, abandoned (originally a legal ceremony acknowledging a
   subordinate relationship)

They surfeited[57] with honey, and began
To loathe the taste of sweetness, whereof a little
More than a little, is by much too much.
So when he had occasion to be seen,

75 He was but as the cuckoo is in June,
Heard, not regarded,[58] seen but with such eyes
As, sick and blunted[59] with community,[60]
Afford[61] no extraordinary gaze,
Such as is bent[62] on sun-like majesty

80 When it shines seldom in admiring[63] eyes,
But rather drowsed,[64] and hung their eye-lids down,
Slept in[65] his face, and rendered such aspect[66]
As cloudy[67] men use to their adversaries,
Being with his presence glutted, gorged, and full.

85 And in that very line,[68] Harry, standest thou,
For thou hast lost thy princely privilege
With[69] vile participation.[70] Not an eye
But is aweary of thy common sight,
Save mine, which hath desired to see thee more,

57 overfed
58 heeded, paid attention to
59 dulled
60 ordinariness, vulgarity
61 yield, furnish, bestow
62 fastened, fixed
63 looking with loving wonder
64 drooping, dulled, drowsy
65 to ("in his presence".)
66 rendered such aspect = giving/reflecting/demonstrating the kind of look/
    appearance/expression (asPECT)
67 glowering, sullen
68 tendency, direction, state of affairs
69 by
70 fellowship, association

Which now doth that I would not have it do,   90
    Make blind itself[71] with foolish tenderness.

Hal   I shall hereafter, my thrice gracious lord,
    Be more myself.

King   For all the world,
    As thou art to this hour was Richard then,
    When I from France set foot at Ravenspurgh,[72]   95
    And even as I was than, is Percy now.
    Now by my scepter, and my soul to boot,
    He hath more worthy interest[73] to the state
    Than thou the shadow[74] of succession.
    For of[75] no right, nor color[76] like to right,   100
    He doth fill fields with harness[77] in the realm,
    Turns head against the lion's armèd jaws,
    And being no more in debt to years than thou
    Leads ancient lords and reverend bishops on
    To bloody battles, and to bruising[78] arms.   105
    What never-dying honor hath he got
    Against renownèd Douglas! Whose high deeds,
    Whose hot incursions,[79] and great name in arms,
    Holds from all soldiers chief majority[80]

---

71 make blind itself = blinds itself with tears
72 Ravenspur, in Yorkshire, N England
73 claim
74 tenuous/ephemeral/delusive faintness/obscurity
75 by, with
76 pretense
77 soldiers ("armament")
78 crushing/mangling/wounding
79 attacks
80 chief majority = primary/highest superiority/preeminence/greatness

110 And military title capital[81]

Through all the kingdoms that acknowledge Christ.

Thrice hath this Hotspur, Mars in swathling clothes,[82]

This infant warrior, in his enterprises[83]

Discomfitèd[84] great Douglas, ta'en him once,

115 Enlarged[85] him, and made a friend of him,

To fill the mouth of deep defiance up,[86]

And shake the peace and safety of our throne.

And what say you to this? Percy, Northumberland,

The Archbishop's Grace[87] of York, Douglas, Mortimer,

120 Capitulate[88] against us, and are up.[89]

But wherefore[90] do I tell these news[91] to thee?

Why, Harry, do I tell thee of my foes,

Which art[92] my nearest and dearest enemy?

Thou that art like[93] enough, through vassal[94] fear,

125 Base inclination,[95] and the start[96] of spleen,

---

81 at the top / head (adjective)
82 swathling clothes = swaddling clothes = cloth wrappings on newborn babies
83 undertakings
84 completely defeated / routed in battle
85 freed him ("set him at large")
86 fill . . . up = satisfy, fulfill, complete
87 formal part of titles, for rulers and in Shakespeare's time for ecclesiastical dignitaries
88 have drawn up articles of agreement
89 up in arms
90 why
91 news: often a plural noun, in Shakespeare's time
92 which art = you who are
93 likely
94 servile, abject
95 reverence, submission
96 sudden rush / fit

To fight against me under Percy's pay,

To dog[97] his heels, and curtsy at his frowns,

To show how much thou art degenerate.[98]

Hal Do not think so, you shall not find it so.

And God forgive them that so much have swayed[99]   130

Your Majesty's good thoughts away from me.

I will redeem all this on Percy's head,

And in the closing of some glorious day

Be bold to tell you that I am your son,

When I will wear a garment all of blood,   135

And stain my favors[100] in a bloody mask

Which, washed away, shall scour my shame with it.[101]

And that shall be the day when, ere it lights,[102]

That this same child of honor and renown,

This gallant Hotspur, this all-praisèd knight,   140

And your unthought-of[103] Harry chance to meet,

For every honor sitting on his[104] helm.

Would they were multitudes, and on my head

My shames redoubled! For the time will come

That I shall make this northern youth exchange   145

His glorious deeds for my indignities.

Percy is but my factor,[105] good my lord,

97 follow like a dog
98 art degenerate = have degenerated/declined/become debased
99 bent, moved, turned
100 (1) features, face, (2) appearance
101 which WASHED aWAY shall SCOUR my SHAME with IT
102 it lights = day comes/arrives
103 unexpected, disregarded
104 Hotspur's
105 agent, usually in business affairs

To engross up[106] glorious deeds on my behalf.
And I will call him to so strict account[107]
150   That he shall render every glory up,[108]
Yea, even the slightest worship[109] of his time,[110]
Or I will tear the reckoning[111] from his heart.
This in the name of God I promise here,
The which if He be pleased I shall perform.
155   I do beseech your Majesty may salve[112]
The long-grown wounds of my intemperance.
If not, the end of life cancels all bands,[113]
And I will die a hundred thousand deaths
Ere break[114] the smallest parcel of this vow.
160   *King* A hundred thousand rebels die in this!
Thou shalt have charge[115] and sovereign trust herein.[116]

ENTER BLUNT

How now, good Blunt? Thy looks are full of speed.
Blunt So hath the business that I come to speak of.
Lord Mortimer[117] of Scotland hath sent word
165   That Douglas and the English rebels met
The eleventh of this month at Shrewsbury.

---

106 engross up = write in large, clear, copybook letters
107 reckoning, calculation*
108 render . . . up = return, repay
109 honor, reputation
110 age, era
111 accounting
112 heal
113 bonds, agreements, debts
114 I break
115 responsibility, office
116 in this matter
117 not the Mortimer of this play

A mighty and a fearful head[118] they are,
If promises be kept on every hand,
As ever offered foul play in a state.[119]

King The Earl of Westmoreland set forth today,   170
With him my son, Lord John of Lancaster,
For this advertisement[120] is five days old.
On Wednesday next, Harry, you shall set forward.
On Thursday we ourselves[121] will march. Our meeting
Is[122] Bridgenorth, and Harry, you shall march   175
Through Gloucestershire,[123] by which account,
Our business valuèd[124] some twelve days hence,
Our general[125] forces at Bridgenorth shall meet.
Our hands are full of business. Let's away,
Advantage feeds him fat, while men delay.   180

EXEUNT

118 front/leading part of an army
119 as EVer OFfered FOUL play IN a STATE
120 warning (adVERtiseMENT)
121 we ourselves = I (the royal "we")
122 will be at
123 GLOsteSHIR
124 appraised/evaluated as of
125 common, whole, collective

SCENE 3

Eastcheap, the Boar's Head Tavern

ENTER FALSTAFF AND BARDOLPH

Falstaff Bardolph, am I not fallen away[1] vilely, since this last
action? Do I not bate?[2] Do I not dwindle? Why, my skin
hangs about me like an old lady's loose gown. I am withered
like an old apple-john.[3] Well, I'll repent, and that suddenly,
5   while I am in some liking.[4] I shall be out of heart[5] shortly,
and then I shall have no strength to repent. And I have not
forgotten what the inside of a church is made of. I am a
peppercorn,[6] a brewer's horse[7] – the inside of a church!
Company, villainous company, hath been the spoil[8] of me.

10 *Bardolph* Sir John, you are so fretful,[9] you cannot live long.

Falstaff Why, there is it. Come, sing me a bawdy song, make
me merry. I was as virtuously given[10] as a gentleman need to
be – virtuous enough. Swore little, diced[11] not above seven
times a week, went to a bawdy house not above once in a
15   quarter – of an hour, paid money that I borrowed – three or

1 fallen away = shrunken, lost flesh
2 (1) lose weight, (2) diminish, lose force
3 shriveled apple, stored for two years
4 in some liking = (1) it pleases me, (2) in good shape / condition
5 out of heart = (1) lose the desire, (2) lose the courage, (3) be out of
condition
6 insignificant, trivial
7 brewer's horse = like a decrepit brewer's horse (brewers' horses generally
were decrepit)
8 spoiling, damaging, destruction
9 irritated, peevish, restless
10 virtuously given = given to virtue
11 gambled with dice

four times, lived well, and in good compass.[12] And now I live
out of all order, out of all compass.

Bardolph Why, you are so fat, Sir John, that you must needs be
out of all compass, out of all reasonable compass, Sir John.

Falstaff Do thou amend thy face, and I'll amend my life. Thou   20
art our admiral,[13] thou bearest the lantern in the poop,[14] but
'tis in the nose of thee. Thou art the knight of the burning lamp.

Bardolph Why, Sir John, my face does you no harm.

Falstaff No, I'll be sworn. I make as good use of it as many a
man doth of a death's head,[15] or a *memento mori*.[16] I never see   25
thy face but I think upon hell-fire, and Dives[17] that lived in
purple, for there he is in his robes, burning, burning. If thou
wert any way given to virtue, I would swear by thy face. My
oath should be "By this fire, that's God's Angel!" But thou art
altogether given over, and wert indeed, but for the light in thy   30
face, the son of utter darkness. When thou ran'st up Gad's Hill
in the night to catch my horse, if I did not think thou hadst
been an *ignis fatuus*,[18] or a ball of wildfire,[19] there's no
purchase[20] in money. O thou art a perpetual triumph,[21] an

---

12 regularity, proportion
13 admiral-ship, flagship
14 stern of a ship
15 death's head = (1) human skull, (2) ring embossed with the image of a
   human skull
16 *memento mori* = "remember that you will die": any reminder of omnipresent
   and inevitable death
17 see Luke 16:19; "Dives" (DIEviz) is Latin for the "rich man" who "was
   clothed in purple" and who goes to hell, while Lazarus,★ a beggar, goes to
   heaven
18 will-o'-the-wisp
19 fireworks
20 gain, profit
21 magnificent victory procession, with torchlights

35 everlasting bonfire[22] light. Thou hast saved me a thousand
marks in links[23] and torches, walking with thee in the night
betwixt tavern and tavern. But the sack that thou hast drunk
me,[24] would have bought me lights as good cheap,[25] at the
dearest chandlers[26] in Europe. I have maintained that
40 salamander[27] of yours with fire[28] any time this two and thirty
years, God reward me for it.

Bardolph 'Sblood, I would my face were in your belly.[29]

Falstaff God-a-mercy,[30] so should I be sure to be
heartburned.[31]

ENTER HOSTESS

45 How now, dame Partlet[32] the hen, have you inquired yet who
picked my pocket?

Hostess Why, Sir John, what do you think, Sir John? Do you
think I keep thieves in my house? I have searched, I have
inquired, so has my husband, man by man, boy by boy, servant
50 by servant. The tithe[33] of a hair was never lost in my house
before.

Falstaff Ye lie, hostess. Bardolph was shaved, and lost many a

---

22 fire for the burning of bones
23 flax stalks soaked in pitch and used as torches
24 drunk me = drunk at my expense ("drunk on me")
25 good cheap = low prices
26 dearest chandlers = most expensive candle makers/sellers
27 lizard thought to live in fire
28 alcohol, ardent spirits
29 were in your belly = I would eat very well indeed (proverbial)
30 God-a-mercy = may God have mercy
31 be heartburned = experience the uneasy, burning feeling of indigestion
32 hen named Pertelote in Chaucer's "Nun's Priest's Tale"
33 tenth part

hair, and I'll be sworn my pocket was picked. Go to, you are a
woman, go.

Hostess Who, I? No, I defy thee. God's light, I was never called   55
so in mine own house before.

Falstaff Go to, I know you well enough.

Hostess No, Sir John, you do not know me, Sir John. I know
you, Sir John, you owe me money, Sir John, and now you pick
a quarrel to beguile me of it. I bought you a dozen of shirts to   60
your back.

Falstaff Dowlas,[34] filthy dowlas. I have given them away to
bakers' wives, they have made bolters[35] of them.

Hostess Now as I am a true woman, holland[36] of eight shillings
an ell![37] You owe money here besides, Sir John, for your   65
diet,[38] and by-drinkings,[39] and money lent you, four and
twenty pounds.

Falstaff He[40] had his part of it, let him pay.

Hostess He? Alas, he is poor, he hath nothing.

Falstaff How? Poor? Look upon his face. What call you rich?   70
Let them coin his nose, let them coin his cheeks – I'll not pay
a denier.[41] What, will you make a younker[42] of me? Shall I
not take mine ease in mine inn, but I shall have my pocket
picked? I have lost a seal ring of my grandfather's, worth forty
mark.   75

34 coarse linen (DAWless)
35 sieves
36 Dutch-made linen
37 1 ell = a yard and a half
38 food
39 drinking apart from and in-between meals
40 Bardolph
41 small copper coin, not worth very much (DIN-ee-ir)
42 (1) fashionable young gentleman, (2) youngster

Hostess   O Jesu, I have heard the prince tell him,[43] I know not
how oft, that that ring was copper.

Falstaff   How? The prince is a Jack, a sneak-up.[44] (*waving a stick*)
'Sblood, and[45] he were here, I would cudgel him like a dog if
80   he would say so.[46]

ENTER HAL, MARCHING. FALSTAFF MEETS HIM,
PLAYING UPON HIS STICK LIKE A FIFE

Falstaff   How now, lad, is the wind in that door?[47] I'faith, must
we all march?

Bardolph   Yea, two, and two, Newgate[48] fashion.

Hostess   My lord, I pray you hear me.

85   **Hal**   What say'st thou, Mistress[49] Quickly? How doth thy
husband? I love him well, he is an honest man.

Hostess   Good my lord, hear me.

Falstaff   Prithee let her alone, and list to me.

Hal   What say'st thou, Jack?

90   **Falstaff**   The other night I fell asleep here, behind the arras, and
had my pocket picked. This house is turned bawdy house,
they pick pockets.

Hal   What didst thou lose, Jack?

Falstaff   Wilt thou believe me, Hal? Three or four bonds of[50]
95   forty pound apiece, and a seal ring of my grandfather's.

---

43 tell him = say
44 (1) mean/servile person, (2) sneak
45 if
46 that
47 is the wind in that door = is that how the wind is blowing?
48 Newgate Prison, to which prisoners were marched, fastened two by two
49 Mrs.
50 bonds of = contracts worth

Hal   A trifle, some eight penny matter.

Hostess So I told him, my lord, and I said I heard your Grace say
so. And my lord he speaks most vilely of you, like a foul-
mouthed man as he is, and said he would cudgel you.

Hal   What? He did not.   100

Hostess There's neither faith, truth, nor womanhood in me
else.

Falstaff There's no more faith in thee than in a stewed prune,[51]
nor no more truth in thee than in a drawn[52] fox, and for
womanhood, Maid Marian[53] may be the deputy's wife[54] of   105
the ward[55] to thee. Go you thing, go.

Hostess Say, what thing, what thing?

Falstaff What thing? Why, a thing to thank God on.[56]

Hostess I am no thing to thank God on, I would thou shouldst
know it, I am an honest man's wife, and setting thy   110
knighthood aside, thou art a knave to call me so.

Falstaff Setting thy womanhood aside, thou art a beast to say
otherwise.

Hostess Say, what beast, thou knave, thou?

Falstaff What beast? Why, an otter.   115

Hal   An otter, Sir John? Why an otter?

Falstaff Why? She's neither fish nor flesh,[57] a man knows not
where to have[58] her.

---

51 stewed prune = bawd, procurer
52 (1) disemboweled, (2) hunted out of cover
53 (1) Robin Hood's woman companion, (2) loose woman in May Day
    country games
54 deputy's wife = wife of the deputy alderman
55 district in a city
56 for
57 animal, beast (whether the otter was fish or mammal was much debated)
58 have sex with

Hostess Thou art an unjust[59] man in saying so, thou or any man
120   knows where to have me, thou knave, thou.

Hal   Thou say'st true, hostess, and he slanders thee most
    grossly.

Hostess   So he doth you, my lord, and said this other day you
    ought[60] him a thousand pound.

125 *Hal*   Sirrah, do I owe you a thousand pound?

Falstaff   A thousand pound, Hal? A million, thy love is worth a
    million. Thou owest me thy love.

Hostess   Nay, my lord, he called you Jack, and said he would
    cudgel you.

130 *Falstaff*   Did I, Bardolph?

Bardolph Indeed, Sir John, you said so.

Falstaff   Yea, if he said my ring was copper.

Hal   I say 'tis copper. Darest thou be as good as thy word
    now?

135 *Falstaff*   Why, Hal, thou knowest as thou art but man I dare, but
    as thou art prince, I fear thee as I fear the roaring of the lion's
    whelp.[61]

Hal   And why not as the lion?

Falstaff   The King himself is to be feared as the lion. Dost thou
140   think I'll fear thee as I fear thy father? Nay, and I do, I pray
    God my girdle break.[62]

Hal   O, if it[63] should, how would thy guts fall about thy
    knees! But sirrah, there's no room for faith, truth, nor honesty

---

59 unfair, dishonest
60 owed
61 cub
62 my girdle break = unmake me (proverbial)
63 i.e., "girdle" in the sense of belt/waistband

in this bosom of thine. It is all filled up with guts and
midriff.[64] Charge an honest woman with picking thy pocket? 145
Why, thou whoreson impudent embossed[65] rascal, if there
were anything in thy pocket but tavern reckonings,
memorandums of bawdy houses, and one poor pennyworth
of sugar candy to make thee long-winded,[66] if thy pocket
were enriched with any other injuries[67] but these, I am a 150
villain. And yet you will stand[68] to it, you will not pocket
up[69] wrong.[70] Art thou not ashamed?

Falstaff Dost thou hear, Hal? Thou knowest in the state of
innocency Adam fell, and what should poor Jack Falstaff do,
in the days of villainy? Thou seest I have more flesh than 155
another man, and therefore more frailty.[71] You confess, then,
you picked my pocket?

Hal   It appears so by the story.[72]

Falstaff Hostess, I forgive thee, go make ready breakfast, love thy
husband, look to[73] thy servants, and cherish thy guests. Thou 160
shalt find me tractable[74] to any honest reason. Thou seest I am
pacified still.[75] Nay, prithee be gone.

EXIT HOSTESS

64 i.e., upper part of the stomach region
65 bulging, swollen (as does a shield, which is embossed)
66 long-winded: fighting cocks were given sugar to increase their endurance
67 things worth stealing (i.e., possible losses)
68 insist on, maintain ("stick to")
69 pocket up = acknowledge, accept
70 i.e., your own wrong-doing
71 i.e., more body = more original sin
72 by the story = from the recital / narrative
73 look to = (1) take care of, pay attention to, (2) beware, be careful of
74 compliant, docile, governable
75 motionless, quiescent, silent

Now Hal, to the news at court. For the robbery, lad, how is
that answered?

165 *Hal* O my sweet beef, I must still be good angel[76] to thee.
The money is paid back again.

Falstaff O I do not like that paying back, 'tis a double labor.

Hal I am good friends with my father, and may do anything

Falstaff Rob me the exchequer, the first thing thou dost, and
170 do it with unwashed hands[77] too.

Bardolph Do, my lord.

Hal I have procured thee, Jack, a charge of foot.

Falstaff I would it had been of horse. Where shall I find one[78]
that can steal well? O, for a fine thief of the age of two and
175 twenty or thereabouts. I am heinously unprovided.[79] Well,
God be thanked for these rebels, they offend none but the
virtuous. I laud them, I praise them.

Hal Bardolph.

Bardolph My lord.

180 *Hal* Go bear this letter to Lord John of Lancaster,
To my brother John. This to my Lord of Westmoreland.

EXIT BARDOLPH

Go Peto, to horse, to horse, for thou and I
Have thirty miles to ride yet ere dinner time.

EXIT PETO

Jack, meet me tomorrow in the Temple Hall

---

76 (1) ministering spirit, (2) gold coin⋆
77 i.e., do not stop even long enough to wash your hands ("right away")
78 someone
79 heinously unprovided = atrociously / infamously not provided / supplied for

At two o'clock in the afternoon.   185
There shalt thou know thy charge, and there receive
Money and order[80] for their furniture.[81]
The land is burning, Percy stands on high,
And either we or they must lower lie.

EXIT HAL

Falstaff Rare words, brave world! Hostess, my breakfast, come!   190
O, I could wish this tavern were my drum.

EXIT FALSTAFF

80 an order, payable by the government
81 fitting out, equipping

Act 4

SCENE I

The rebel camp, near Shrewsbury

ENTER HOTSPUR, DOUGLAS, AND WORCESTER

Hotspur. Well said, my noble Scot. If speaking truth
  In this fine[1] age were not thought flattery,
  Such attribution[2] should the Douglas have
  As not a soldier of this season's stamp[3]
5 Should go so general current through the world.
  By God, I cannot flatter, I do defy
  The tongues of soothers,[4] but a braver place
  In my heart's love hath no man than your self.
  Nay, task me[5] to my word. Approve[6] me, lord.
10 *Douglas* Thou art the king of honor.

---

1 superior (here, used negatively)
2 reputation
3 stamping, impressing (usually on metal)
4 flatterers
5 task me = put to the proof
6 test

No man[7] so potent[8] breathes upon the ground[9]
But I will beard[10] him.

Hotspur   Do so, and 'tis well.

ENTER MESSENGER BEARING LETTERS[11]

                          (*to Messenger*) What letters hast
thou there?

(*to Douglas*) I can but thank you.

Messenger These letters come from your father.

Hotspur   Letters from
him?   15

Why comes he not himself?

Messenger He cannot come, my lord, he is grievous sick.

Hotspur   Zounds, how has he the leisure to be sick
In such a justling[12] time? Who leads his power?
Under whose government come they along?   20

Messenger His letters bears[13] his mind, not I his mind.

Worcester (*to Messenger*) I prithee tell me, doth he keep[14] his
bed?

Messenger He did, my lord, four days ere I set forth,
And at the time of my departure thence

---

7 no man = there is no one
8 powerful
9 breathes upon the ground = alive
10 boldly oppose
11 (?) plural? singular?
12 justling = pushing, shoving, struggling, colliding
13 N.B.: 7 lines earlier, the Messenger says "letters come" (plural noun and verb);
   here he says "letters bears" (plural noun, singular verb); both constructions
   were permissible in Shakespeare's time
14 take to/stay in (past and present tense are not as clearly distinguished, in
   Shakespeare's English, as they have come to be)

25 He was much feared[15] by his physicians.

Worcester   I would the state of time[16] had first been whole,[17]

Ere he by sickness had been visited.[18]

His health was never better[19] worth than now.

Hotspur   Sick now?[20] Droop[21] now? This sickness doth infect

30 The very lifeblood of our enterprise,

'Tis catching[22] hither even to our camp.

He writes me here that inward sickness,[23]

And that his friends by deputation[24]

Could not so soon be drawn,[25] nor did he think it meet[26]

35 To lay so dangerous and dear[27] a trust

On any soul removed[28] but[29] on his own.

Yet doth he give us bold advertisement

That with our small conjunction we should on,[30]

To see how fortune is disposed to us.

40 For as he writes, there is no quailing[31] now,

Because the King is certainly possessed[32]

15 feared for
16 state of time = condition of the times
17 in good/sound condition
18 afflicted, assailed
19 of better
20 be sick NOW?
21 sink down, decline, languish
22 infecting, communicating
23 (?) two words possibly omitted: "stays him" (?)
24 by deputation = by anyone delegated to act on his behalf
25 moved, gathered
26 proper, appropriate
27 glorious, honorable
28 (adjective modifying "soul") distant in relationship
29 but only
30 carry/go on
31 giving way, becoming faint-hearted
32 aware

Of all our purposes. What say you to it?

Worcester   Your father's sickness is a maim[33] to us.

Hotspur   A perilous gash,[34] a very limb lopped off,

And yet in faith it is not. His present want[35]   45

Seems more than we shall find it. Were it good

To set the exact wealth[36] of all our states

All at one cast?[37] To set so rich a main[38]

On the nice[39] hazard[40] of one doubtful hour?

It were not good, for therein should we read[41]   50

The very bottom[42] and the soul[43] of hope,

The very list,[44] the very utmost bound[45]

Of all our fortunes.

Douglas   Faith, and so we should,

Where now remains[46] a sweet reversion.[47]

We may boldly spend upon the hope   55

Of what 'tis to come in.

A comfort[48] of retirement[49] lives in this.

33 injury, mutilation, loss
34 cut, cleft, wound
35 his present want = doing without/lacking him now
36 exact wealth = precise/rigorous prosperity
37 throw (as of dice)
38 number called/set in the dice game known as hazard, before the dice are thrown
39 foolish
40 (1) risk, chance, (2) dice game called "hazard" (see n. 38)
41 make out, discover, see, predict
42 deepest part, foundation, basis
43 fundamental essence/element
44 boundary, limit
45 very utmost bound = truly, the furthest boundary
46 there is still left
47 property/money to become available in the future (reeVERzeeOWN)
48 support, strength, delight
49 withdrawal, retreat

Hotspur A rendezvous,[50] a home to fly[51] unto,

  If that the Divel and mischance look big[52]

60 Upon the maidenhead[53] of our affairs.

Worcester But yet I would your father had been here.

  The quality[54] and hair[55] of our attempt

  Brooks no division.[56] It will be thought

  By some that know not why he is away

65 That wisdom, loyalty, and mere[57] dislike

  Of our proceedings kept the Earl from hence.

  And think how such an apprehension[58]

  May turn the tide of fearful faction,[59]

  And breed a kind of question[60] in our cause.

70 For well you know we of the off'ring[61] side

  Must keep aloof from strict arbitrement,[62]

  And stop[63] all sight-holes, every loop,[64] from whence

  The eye of reason may pry[65] in upon us.

50 assembly point
51 run, flee
52 look big = present themselves/seem to us (1) haughty, arrogant, (2) great, important
53 early/first stages/tests
54 (1) skill, (2) excellence, (3) manner, character, (4) origin, cause
55 (1) detail, (2) nature
56 brooks no division = hold/tolerates/permits* no partitioning/separations/ discords/dissensions (diVIzeeOWN)
57 unmixed, pure, absolute
58 perception, idea, opinion (APpreeHENseeOWN)
59 fearful faction = timid/frightened (1) conduct, behavior, acting, (2) class, sections, set of persons, (3) partisans, parties (FAXseeOWN)
60 controversy, dispute
61 proposing ("candidate-like")
62 (1) decision-making, (2) freedom of choice (arBItriMENT)
63 plug
64 opening in a wall
65 look, peer

This absence of your father's draws[66] a curtain
That shows the ignorant[67] a kind of fear   75
Before not dreamt of.

Hotspur   You strain[68] too far.
I rather of his absence make this use:
It lends a luster and more great opinion,
A larger dare to our great enterprise
Than if the Earl were here, for men must think   80
If we without his help can make a head[69]
To push against a kingdom, with his help
We shall o'erturn it topsy-turvy down.
Yet[70] all goes well, yet all our joints are whole.

Douglas   As heart[71] can think, there is not such a word   85
Spoke of in Scotland as this term[72] of fear.

ENTER VERNON

Hotspur My cousin Vernon, welcome by my soul.
Vernon   Pray God my news be worth a welcome, lord.
The Earl of Westmoreland, seven thousand strong,
Is marching hitherwards, with him Prince John.   90
Hotspur No harm. What more?
Vernon   And further, I have learned,
The King himself in person is[73] set forth,

66 pulls back, opens
67 uninformed
68 press, force
69 make a head = (1) advance, press forward, (2) raise an army
70 as yet
71 as heart = as far as mind
72 word
73 has

Or hitherwards intended[74] speedily,

With strong and mighty preparation.[75]

95 *Hotspur* He shall be welcome too. Where is his son,

The nimble-footed madcap Prince of Wales,

And his comrades that daft[76] the world aside

And bid it pass?

Vernon   All furnished,[77] all in arms,

All plumed like estridges[78] that with the wind

100 Baited,[79] like eagles having lately bathed,

Glittering in golden coats like images,[80]

As full of spirit as the month of May,

And gorgeous[81] as the sun at midsummer,

Wanton as[82] youthful goats, wild as young bulls.

105 I saw young Harry with his beaver[83] on,

His cushes[84] on his thighs, gallantly armed,

Rise from the ground like feathered Mercury,

And vaulted[85] with such ease into his seat[86]

As if an angel dropped down from the clouds

74 intending, meaning
75 forces (PREpaRAYseeOWN)
76 throw / threw (daff = to throw off)
77 equipped★
78 ostriches
79 (?) (1) (as here punctuated, and as interpreted by most editors) fluttered their
   wings, *or* (2) (differently punctuated) "like estridges that, with the wind /
   bated, [abated, lessened]); the verb of which "estridges" is the subject then
   becomes "wanton," 4 lines further along
80 painted pictures / statues
81 showy, magnificent, brilliant
82 (verb) wanton as = sport / frolic like
83 face guard on a helmet
84 thigh-piece armor (cuisse)
85 mount by leaping into the saddle (impressive, given the weight of full armor)
86 saddle

To turn and wind[87] a fiery Pegasus,[88]   110
And witch[89] the world with noble horsemanship.
Hotspur   No more, no more, worse than the sun in March.[90]
This praise doth nourish[91] agues. Let them come.
They come like sacrifices in their trim,[92]
And to the fire-eyed maid of smoky war,   115
All hot, and bleeding, will we offer them.
The mailèd Mars[93] shall on his altars sit
Up to the ears in blood. I am on fire
To hear this rich reprisal[94] is so nigh,
And yet not ours. Come, let me taste[95] my horse,   120
Who is to bear me like a thunderbolt
Against the bosom of the Prince of Wales.
Harry to Harry shall, hot horse to horse,
Meet and ne'er part till one drop down a corse.[96]
O that Glendower were come.
Vernon   There is more news.   125
I learned in Worcester, as I rode along,
He[97] cannot draw his power this[98] fourteen days.
Douglas   That's the worst tidings that I hear of yet.

---

87 turn and wind: terms used in horsemanship (wind [rhymes with "bind,"
    "find"] = wheel about)
88 mythical winged horse
89 bewitch, put a spell on
90 thought to produce agues
91 (1) cultivate, nourish, grow, (2) feed, support
92 array, dress, appearance
93 mailèd Mars = god of war, wearing mail/armor
94 prize
95 (1) handle, touch, feel, (2) test, (3) recognize
96 corpse
97 Glendower
98 for

Worcester   Ay, by my faith, that bears a frosty[99] sound.

130 *Hotspur*   What may the King's whole battle[100] reach unto?

Vernon   To[101] thirty thousand.

Hotspur   Forty let it be.

My father and Glendower being both away,

The powers of us may serve so great a day.

Come, let us take a muster[102] speedily.

135   Doom's day is near. Die all, die merrily.

Douglas   Talk not of dying, I am[103] out of fear

Of death, or death's hand, for this one half year.

EXEUNT

99 chilling
100 army, forces ready for war
101 as much as
102 inspection, military review
103 have been

SCENE 2

A road near Coventry

ENTER FALSTAFF AND BARDOLPH

Falstaff Bardolph, get thee before to Coventry, fill me a bottle
of sack. Our soldiers shall march through. We'll to Sutton
Co'fill[1] tonight.

Bardolph Will you give me money, captain?

Falstaff Lay out,[2] lay out.   5

Bardolph This bottle makes[3] an angel.

Falstaff And if it do, take it for thy labor. And if it make twenty
take them all, I'll answer[4] the coinage.[5] Bid my Lieutenant
Peto meet me at town's end.

Bardolph I will, captain. Farewell.   10

EXIT

Falstaff If I be not ashamed of my soldiers, I am a soused
gurnet.[6] I have misused the King's press[7] damnably. I have got
in exchange of a hundred and fifty soldiers three hundred and
odd pounds. I press me none but good householders,[8]
yeomen's[9] sons, inquire me out[10] contracted[11] bachelors,   15

1 Coldfield
2 spend it
3 brings the total advanced so far to
4 be responsible for
5 making of more money: (1) via Hal, (2) via counterfeit coinage?
6 soused gurnet = pickled big-headed fish (negative)
7 compulsorily taking of men into military service
8 i.e., substantial citizens, since Falstaff first conscripts them and then has them
  pay him to take someone else instead
9 country man owning farmland
10 inquire me out = look/search for
11 engaged to be married

such as had been asked twice on the banns,[12] such a
commodity of warm[13] slaves as had as lief[14] hear the Divel as
a drum, such as fear the report of a caliver[15] worse than a
struck[16] fowl or a hurt wild duck. I pressed me none but such
toasts and butter, with hearts in their bellies no bigger than
pins' heads, and they have bought out[17] their services.[18] And
now my whole charge consists of ancients,[19] corporals,
lieutenants, gentlemen[20] of companies, slaves as ragged as
Lazarus in the painted cloth,[21] where[22] the glutton's dogs
licked his sores,[23] and[24] such as indeed were never soldiers,
but discarded, unjust[25] servingmen, younger sons to younger
brothers,[26] revolted tapsters,[27] and ostlers, tradefallen,[28] the
cankers of[29] a calm world and a long peace, ten times more

12 i.e., the public proclamation of marriage ("bann") had taken place the
   required number of times and the marriage thereby became imminent
13 comfortable, prosperous
14 as lief = rather
15 light musket ("rifle")
16 wounded, stricken
17 bought out = ransomed, gotten rid of
18 military service
19 ensigns, standard-bearers (in *Othello,* Iago is Othello's ancient)
20 an uncertain rank, higher than enlisted men, lower than officers
21 in the painted cloth = pictures inexpensively painted directly onto cloth
22 in which, when
23 Luke 16:31, "the dogs came and licked his sores"
24 and also
25 dishonest
26 to younger brothers = the younger sons of those who had been younger
   brothers themselves, and under English law had therefore inherited nothing
   (primogeniture requiring that everything went to the oldest son)
27 revolted tapsters = indentured barkeepers who had run away from their
   contracted-for apprenticeships
28 bankrupt
29 cankers of = worms/ulcerous sores produced by

dishonorable[30] ragged than an old fazed[31] ancient. And such
have I to[32] fill up the rooms[33] of them as have bought out 30
their[34] services, that you would think that I had a hundred
and fifty tottered prodigals,[35] lately come from swine-
keeping, from eating draff[36] and husks. A mad fellow met me
on the way, and told me I had unloaded all the gibbets,[37] and
pressed the dead bodies. No eye hath seen such scarecrows. 35
I'll not march through Coventry with them, that's flat. Nay,
and[38] the villains march wide betwixt the legs[39] as if they had
gyves[40] on, for indeed I had the most of them out of prison,
there's not a shirt and a half[41] in all my company, and the half
shirt is two napkins tacked[42] together, and thrown over the 40
shoulders like a herald's coat[43] without sleeves, and the shirt,
to say the truth, stolen from my host at Saint Albans, or the
red-nose innkeeper of Daventry.[44] But that's all one, they'll

30 dishonorably
31 worn out
32 in order to
33 places / spaces on the impressment list
34 their own
35 tottered prodigals = tattered (1) prodigal sons, (2) spendthrifts, bankrupts
36 swine-swill, dregs left over after brewing
37 (1) gallows, (2) brackets on which hanged bodies, after death, were publicly
    displayed
38 and also
39 wide betwixt the legs = with their legs wide apart
40 shackles, chains
41 and a half = plus an undershirt
42 napkins tacked = small towels fastened / hastily sewed
43 "heralds / That cryen rich folk's laudes [praise]". . . / Had on him thrown
    a vesture [garment] / Which that men clepe [call] a coat armure [cloth tunic
    worn over armor]" (Chaucer House of Fame 1321–26)
44 Saint Albans . . . Daventry = towns on the road from London to Coventry

find linen[45] enough on every hedge.[46]

ENTER HAL AND WESTMORELAND

45   *Hal*   How now, blown[47] Jack? How now, quilt?[48]

     Falstaff   What Hal, how now, mad wag? What a divel dost thou in Warwickshire? My good Lord of Westmoreland, I cry you mercy, I thought your honor had already been at[49] Shrewsbury.

50   *Westmoreland* Faith, Sir John, 'tis more than time that I were there, and you too, but my powers are there already. The King I can tell you looks for us all. We must away all tonight.[50]

     Falstaff   Tut, never fear[51] me, I am as vigilant as a cat to steal[52] cream.

55   *Hal*   I think to steal cream indeed, for thy theft hath already made thee butter. But tell me, Jack, whose fellows are these that come after?[53]

     Falstaff   Mine, Hal, mine.

     Hal   I did never see such pitiful rascals.

60   *Falstaff*   Tut, tut, good enough to toss.[54] Food for powder,[55] food for powder. They'll fill a pit[56] as well as

---

45 clothing, including both shirts and undershirts
46 i.e, where they were spread out for drying (and can therefore be stolen)
47 (1) out of breath, (2) swollen, inflated
48 i.e., well-padded
49 been at = reached, come to
50 Quarto: night; Folio: tonight
51 fear for
52 to steal = stealing
53 behind you
54 back and forth? at spear point? toss away?
55 gunpowder ("cannon fodder")
56 i.e., as corpses

better.[57] Tush, man, mortal men, mortal men.

Westmoreland Ay, but Sir John, methinks they are exceeding
poor and bare,[58] too beggarly.

Falstaff   Faith, for their poverty I know not where they   65
had[59] that, and for their bareness I am sure they never learned
that of me.

Hal   No, I'll be sworn, unless you call three fingers[60] in
the ribs bare. But sirrah, make haste, Percy is already in the
field.   70

EXIT HAL

Falstaff   What, is the King encamped?[61]

Westmoreland He is, Sir John. I fear we shall stay[62] too long.

EXIT WESTMORELAND

Falstaff   Well,
To[63] the latter end[64] of a fray, and the beginning of a feast,
Fits a dull fighter and a keen[65] guest.   75

EXIT FALSTAFF

57 better men
58 (1) lean, (2) naked
59 obtained, got
60 as wide as three fingers' width
61 in camp
62 linger
63 to be going to
64 latter end = last part
65 bold

SCENE 3

Shrewsbury, the rebel camp

ENTER HOTSPUR, WORCESTER, DOUGLAS, AND VERNON

Hotspur We'll fight with him tonight.

Worcester   It may not be.

Douglas You give him then advantage.

Vernon   Not a whit.

Hotspur Why say you so? Looks he not for supply?[1]

Vernon So do we.

Hotspur   His is certain, ours is doubtful.

5 *Worcester* Good cousin, be advised,[2] stir not tonight.

Vernon Do not, my lord.

Douglas   You do not counsel well.

You speak it out of fear, and cold heart.[3]

Vernon Do me no slander, Douglas. By my life —

And I dare well maintain[4] it with my life —

10 If well-respected[5] honor bid me on,

I hold as little counsel with weak fear

As you, my lord, or any Scot that this day lives.

Let it be seen tomorrow in the battle

Which of us fears.

Douglas   Yea, or tonight.

Vernon   Content.[6]

15 *Hotspur* Tonight, say I.

1 assistance, relief, reinforcements
2 (1) warned, (2) cautious, wary
3 cold heart = lack of ardor/enthusiasm
4 preserve, support, back up, uphold
5 well-respected = well-considered
6 enough, be satisfied

Vernon   Come, come, it may not be. I wonder much,
    Being men of such great leading[7] as you are,
    That you foresee not what impediments
    Drag back our expedition.[8] Certain horse[9]
    Of my cousin Vernon's are not yet come up,   20
    Your uncle Worcester's horse came but today,
    And now their pride and mettle is asleep,
    Their courage with hard labor tame[10] and dull
    That not a horse is half the half of himself.

Hotspur   So are the horses[11] of the enemy   25
    In general journey-bated[12] and brought low.[13]
    The better part of ours are full of rest.

Worcester The number of the King exceedeth our.[14]
    For God's sake, cousin, stay till all come in.

THE TRUMPET SOUNDS[15] A PARLEY[16]

ENTER SIR WALTER BLUNT

Blunt   I come with gracious offers from the King,   30
    If you vouchsafe me hearing, and respect.[17]

Hotspur   Welcome, Sir Walter Blunt. And would to God

7 generalship, experience of command
8 drag back our expedition = retard/delay our speedy performance/
  accomplishment
9 cavalry soldiers/men
10 so tame
11 cavalrymen
12 in general journey-bated = nearly all travel-lessened/weakened
13 weak, dull
14 Quarto: our; Folio: ours
15 announces
16 temporary truce for discussion with an enemy
17 consideration

You were of our determination![18]
Some of us love you well, and even those some
35 Envy[19] your great deservings and good name,
Because you are not of our quality,[20]
But stand against us like an enemy.

Blunt And God defend[21] but still I should stand so,
So long as out of limit[22] and true rule[23]
40 You stand against anointed[24] majesty.
But to my charge. The King hath sent to know
The nature of your griefs[25] and whereupon[26]
You conjure[27] from the breast of civil peace
Such bold hostility, teaching his duteous land
45 Audacious cruelty.[28] If that the King
Have any way[29] your good deserts[30] forgot,
Which he confesseth to be manifold,
He bids you name your griefs, and with all speed
You shall have your desires, with interest,
50 And pardon absolute for yourself and these
Herein misled by your suggestion.[31]

---

18 opinion, position (deeTERmiNAseeOWN)
19 begrudge you
20 party, side
21 prevent, forbid, prohibit
22 out of limit = beyond/outside of limitations/restrictions
23 (1) self-regulation/governance, discipline, (2) custom, habit, law
24 consecrated, sacred
25 sufferings★
26 upon what, wherefore/why
27 conspire, plan by conspiracy
28 audacious cruelty = bold/daring/wicked/shameless hard-heartedness/
   indifference to pain/suffering/misery
29 any way = in any way
30 deserving, worthiness
31 prompting, incitement (suJESteeOWN)

Hotspur   The King is kind, and well we know the King
    Knows at what time to promise, when to pay.
    My father, and my uncle, and myself
    Did give him that same royalty he wears,   55
    And when he was not six-and-twenty strong,
    Sick[32] in the world's regard, wretched and low,
    A poor unminded[33] outlaw sneaking home,
    My father gave him welcome to the shore.
    And when he heard him swear and vow to God   60
    He came but to be Duke of Lancaster,
    To sue his livery,[34] and beg his peace
    With tears of innocency, and terms of zeal,[35]
    My father, in kind heart and pity moved,
    Swore him assistance, and performed it, too.   65
    Now when the lords and barons of the realm
    Perceived Northumberland[36] did lean to him,
    The more and less[37] came in with cap and knee,[38]
    Met him in boroughs, cities, villages,
    Attended him on bridges, stood in lanes,   70
    Laid gifts before him, proffered him their oaths,
    Gave him their heirs as pages, followed him,
    Even at the heels, in golden[39] multitudes.

32 (1) weak, (2) ailing, not well
33 disregarded, unnoticed
34 sue his livery = petition for his property/inheritance, appropriated by the
    then King
35 of zeal = ardent, devout★
36 Hotspur's father
37 great and not-so-great
38 with cap and knee = doffing their hats and bowing their knees
39 (1) very favorable, (2) joyous

He presently, as greatness knows[40] itself,

75 Steps me a little higher than his vow

Made to my father, while his blood was poor,

Upon the naked shore at Ravenspurgh,

And now, forsooth, takes on him to reform

Some certain[41] edicts, and some strait[42] decrees,

80 That lie too heavy on the commonwealth,

Cries out upon[43] abuses, seems to weep

Over his country's[44] wrongs, and by this face,[45]

This seeming brow of justice, did he win

The hearts of all that he did angle[46] for.

85 Proceeded further, cut me off the heads

Of all the favorites that the absent[47] King

In deputation[48] left[49] behind him here,

When he was personal[50] in the Irish war.

Blunt   Tut, I came not to hear this.

Hotspur   Then to the point.

90 In short time after he deposed the King,

Soon after that deprived him of his life,

And in the neck of[51] that tasked[52] the whole state,

40 comes to know/understand/feel
41 settled, fixed
42 rigorous
43 at
44 Folio: country's; Quarto: country
45 appearance, pretense
46 fish
47 then-absent
48 in deputation = as his deputed representatives
49 had left
50 engaged in person
51 in the neck of = immediately after
52 taxed, exacted tribute from

To make that worse, suffered[53] his kinsman March[54]
(Who is, if every owner were well placed,[55]
Indeed his[56] King) to be engaged[57] in Wales,   95
There without ransom to lie forfeited,
Disgraced me in my happy[58] victories,
Sought to entrap me by intelligence,[59]
Rated[60] mine uncle from the council board,[61]
In rage dismissed my father from the court,   100
Broke oath on oath, committed wrong on wrong,
And in conclusion drove us to seek out
This head[62] of safety,[63] and withal to pry
Into his title, the which we find
Too indirect[64] for long continuance.   105
Blunt   Shall I return this answer to the King?
Hotspur Not so, Sir Walter. We'll withdraw a while.[65]
Go to the King, and let there be impawned[66]
Some surety for a safe return again,
And in the morning early shall mine uncle   110
Bring him our purposes. And so farewell.

53 permitted, allowed★
54 Mortimer
55 if every owner were well placed = if everyone who owned something had proper possession thereof
56 the King's
57 held as a pledge★ ("hostage")
58 fortunate
59 spying
60 drove off / away
61 table
62 (1) source, fountainhead, (2) army, force
63 our (the rebels') safety, a safeguard / protection
64 crooked, deceitful, corrupt
65 a while = for some time
66 pledged (i.e., left with the rebels, as hostage for the rebel emissary's security)

Blunt   I would you would accept of⁶⁷ grace and love.

Hotspur And maybe so we shall.

Blunt   Pray God you do.

EXEUNT

67 out of

SCENE 4 ·

York, the Archbishop's palace

ENTER ARCHBISHOP AND SIR MICHAEL

Archbishop Hie,[1] good Sir Michael, bear this sealèd brief[2]
With wingèd haste to the Lord Marshall,[3]
This to my cousin Scroop,[4] and all the rest
To whom they are directed. If you knew
How much they do import, you would make haste.   5
Sir Michael My good lord, I guess their tenor.[5]
Archbishop   Like enough
you do.
Tomorrow, good Sir Michael, is a day
Wherein the fortune of ten thousand men
Must bide[6] the touch.[7] For sir, at Shrewsbury,
As I am truly given to understand,   10
The King with mighty and quick-raisèd power
Meets with Lord Harry. And I fear, Sir Michael,
What with the sickness of Northumberland,
Whose power was in the first proportion,[8]
And what with Owen Glendower's absence thence,   15
Who, with[9] them, was a rated sinew[10] too,
And comes not in, overruled by prophecies,

1 hurry
2 letter
3 another rebel leader, the Duke of Norfolk, not a character in this play
4 not identifiable
5 general sense/substance/purpose*
6 await
7 (1) contact, blows, (2) test, proof
8 quantity, number (proPORseeOWN)
9 along with
10 rated sinew = valued strength, force ("muscle")

I fear the power of Percy is too weak
To wage an instant trial[11] with the King.
20 *Sir Michael* Why, my good lord, you need not fear,
There is Douglas, and Lord Mortimer.
Archbishop No, Mortimer is not there.
Sir Michael But there is Mordake, Vernon, Lord Harry Percy.
And there is my Lord of Worcester, and a head
25 Of gallant warriors, noble gentlemen.
Archbishop And so there is. But yet the King hath drawn
The special head[12] of all the land together,
The Prince of Wales, Lord John of Lancaster,
The noble Westmoreland, and warlike Blunt,
30 And many mo[13] corivals and dear[14] men [15]
Of estimation[16] and command[17] in arms.
Sir Michael Doubt not, my lord. They shall be well opposed.
Archbishop I hope no less, yet needful 'tis to fear,
And to prevent the worst, Sir Michael, speed.
35 For if Lord Percy thrive not, ere the King
Dismiss his power he[18] means to visit us,
For he hath heard of our confederacy,[19]
And 'tis but wisdom to make strong against him.
Therefore make haste. I must go write again
40 To other friends. And so farewell, Sir Michael.

EXEUNT

11 battle, military contest*
12 (1) men, (2) heads, leaders, chiefs
13 more
14 (1) bold, hardy, (2) glorious
15 (and MAny MO coRIvals AND dear MEN)
16 esteem, reputation
17 ability to command
18 the King
19 alliance, conspiracy

Act 5

SCENE I

Shrewsbury, the King's camp

ENTER THE KING, HAL, LORD JOHN OF LANCASTER,
SIR WALTER BLUNT, AND FALSTAFF

King How bloodily the sun begins to peer
  Above yon bulky[1] hill. The day looks pale
  At[2] his distemperature.[3]
Hal   The southern wind
  Doth play the trumpet[4] to his[5] purposes,
  And by his hollow whistling in the leaves
  Foretells a tempest[6] and a blust'ring day.   5
King Then with the losers let it sympathize,
  For nothing can seem foul to those that win.

---

1 Quarto: bulky; Folio: busky
2 because of
3 his distemperature = the sun's disordered / disturbed state / condition
4 play the trumpet = provide the music
5 to his = for / to the tune of the sun's
6 rainstorm

THE TRUMPET SOUNDS

ENTER WORCESTER AND VERNON

King   How now, my Lord of Worcester. 'Tis not well

10   That you and I should meet upon such terms

As now we meet. You have deceived our trust,

And made us doff[7] our easy robes of peace,

To crush our old limbs in ungentle[8] steel.

This is not well, my lord, this is not well.

15   What say you to it? Will you again unknit[9]

This churlish[10] knot of all-abhorrèd war?

And[11] move in that obedient orb[12] again,

Where you did give a fair and natural light,

And be no more an exhaled[13] meteor,

20   A prodigy[14] of fear, and a portent

Of broachèd mischief[15] to the unborn times?

Worcester Hear me, my liege.

For mine own part I could be well content

To entertain the lag[16] end of my life

25   With quiet hours. For I protest

I have not sought the day of this dislike.[17]

7 put/take off
8 hard, rough, rugged
9 untie
10 brutal, hard, harsh, violent
11 rather than (see *OED*, and, conj., 2)
12 obedient orb = dutiful/submissive ring/circle (modern "orbit" was not yet in use)
13 blown off, breathed forth
14 portent, omen
15 broachèd mischief = set-into-motion distress/trouble/misfortune
16 hindmost ("dregs")
17 (1) discord, disagreement, (2) displeasure, repugnance

King	You have not sought it. How comes it then?
Falstaff	Rebellion lay in his way, and he found it.
Hal	Peace, chewet,[18] peace.

Worcester It pleased your Majesty to turn your looks   30
    Of favor from myself, and all our house.
    And yet I must remember[19] you, my lord,
    We were the first and dearest of your friends.
    For you my staff of office did I break[20]
    In Richard's time, and posted[21] day and night   35
    To meet you on the way, and kiss your hand,
    When yet you were in place and in account[22]
    Nothing[23] so strong and fortunate as I.
    It was myself, my brother, and his son,
    That brought you home, and boldly did outdare   40
    The dangers of the time. You swore to us,
    And you did swear that oath at Doncaster,
    That you did nothing purpose 'gainst the state,
    Nor claim no further than your new-fall'n[24] right,
    The seat[25] of Gaunt, dukedom of Lancaster.   45
    To this we swore our aid. But in short space
    It rained down fortune show'ring on your head,
    And such a flood of greatness fell on you,
    What with our help, what with the absent King,

18 jackdaw, chattering crow
19 remind
20 i.e., not literal: Worcester broke his vow of allegiance to Henry IV's
    predecessor
21 traveled rapidly (via postings of frequently changed horses)
22 reputation
23 nowhere near
24 new-fall'n = new-born (i.e., by the death of his father, John of Gaunt)
25 place, situation

50   What with the injuries[26] of a wanton time,
The seeming sufferances[27] that you had borne,
And the contrarious[28] winds that held the King
So long in his unlucky Irish wars
That all in England did repute him dead.
55   And from this swarm of fair advantages
You took occasion to be quickly wooed
To gripe[29] the general sway[30] into your hand,
Forgot your oath to us at Doncaster,
And being fed by us, you used us so
60   As[31] that ungentle gull,[32] the cuckoo's bird,
Useth the sparrow, did oppress[33] our nest,
Grew by our feeding to so great a bulk
That even our love durst not come near your sight,
For fear of swallowing. But with nimble wing
65   We were enforced for safety sake to fly
Out of your sight, and raise this present head,
Whereby we stand opposed by such means
As you yourself have forged against yourself,
By unkind usage,[34] dangerous countenance,
70   And violation of all faith and troth,[35]
Sworn to us in your younger enterprise.

---

26 wrongs, violations
27 suffering
28 hostile, unpredictable, perverse
29 grasp, clutch, seize
30 sovereign power/authority
31 so as = like
32 ungentle gull = unmannerly/discourteous/ignoble young bird/fledgling
33 did oppress = you did trample/crush/injure
34 unkind usage = unnatural/unpleasant/ungracious treatment
35 loyalty, good faith

King These things indeed you have articulate,[36]
    Proclaimed at market crosses,[37] read in churches,
    To face[38] the garment of rebellion
    With some fine color that may please the eye   75
    Of fickle changelings[39] and poor discontents,
    Which[40] gape and rub the elbow[41] at the news
    Of hurly-burly[42] innovation.[43]
    And never yet did insurrection want
    Such water colors to impaint[44] his cause,   80
    Nor moody[45] beggars starving[46] for a time
    Of pell-mell havoc[47] and confusion.
Hal In both your armies there is many a soul
    Shall pay full dearly for this encounter,
    If once they[48] join in trial. Tell your nephew   85
    The Prince of Wales doth join with all the world
    In praise of Henry Percy. By my hopes
    (This present enterprise set off[49] his head)
    I do not think a braver gentleman,
    More active, valiant, or more valiant young,   90

---

36 (verb, past tense) expressed, charged
37 market crosses = crosses erected at prominent locations in marketplaces
38 put a bold/false face on
39 waverers, turncoats, renegades
40 who
41 rub the elbow = chuckle
42 hurly-burly = tumultuous, confused
43 (1) novelties, (2) rebelliousness (of HURleeBERlee INoVAYseeOWN)
44 depict, show, portray
45 obstinate, willful, angry
46 hungry, longing
47 pell-mell havoc = confused/headlong pillage/plundering
48 the two armies
49 set off = removed/canceled from

More daring, or more bold, is now alive

To grace this latter age with noble deeds.

For my part, I may speak it to my shame,

I have a truant been to chivalry,

95   And so I hear he doth account me too.

Yet this before my father's majesty:

I am content that he shall take the odds[50]

Of his great name and estimation,

And will, to save the blood on either side,

100   Try[51] fortune with him in a single fight.

King And Prince of Wales, so dare we venture[52] thee,

Albeit, considerations infinite

Do make[53] against it. No, good Worcester, no,

We love our people well, even those we love[54]

105   That are misled upon your cousin's part,

And will they[55] take the offer of our grace,

Both he, and they, and you, yea, every man

Shall be my friend again, and I'll be his.

So tell your cousin, and bring me word

110   What he will do. But if he will not yield,

Rebuke[56] and dread correction[57] wait on[58] us,

And they shall do their office.[59] So be gone.

---

50 take the odds = take the advantage
51 test
52 risk
53 exist
54 even those we love = we love even those
55 and will they = if they will
56 disgrace, shame★
57 punishment
58 wait on = (1) watch over, take care / charge of, (2) serve, attend on, (3) wait for
59 duty

We will not now be troubled with reply,
We offer fair,[60] take it advisedly.[61]

EXIT WORCESTER

Hal   It will not be accepted, on my life.   115
The Douglas and the Hotspur both together
Are confident against the world in arms.
King   Hence, therefore, every leader to his charge,
For on their answer will we set on them,
And God befriend us, as[62] our cause is just.   120

EXEUNT ALL BUT HAL AND FALSTAFF

Falstaff Hal, if thou see me down in the battle,
And bestride[63] me, so,[64] 'tis a point[65] of friendship.
Hal   Nothing but a colossus[66] can do thee that friendship.
Say thy prayers, and farewell.
Falstaff I would 'twere bedtime, Hal, and all well.   125
Hal   Why, thou owest God a death.[67]

EXIT HAL

Falstaff 'Tis not due yet. I would be loath to pay Him before his
day.[68] What need I be so forward with him that calls[69] not on

60 (1) kindly, civilly, (2) justly, honestly, (3) favorably, auspiciously
61 wisely, judiciously
62 (1) to the extent that, *or* (2), because, whereas
63 and if you stand over me, legs astride
64 like this (demonstrating, legs apart)
65 item, aspect, quality, instance, action
66 huge statue of a man (the colossus of Rhodes, one of the seven wonders of
    the ancient world, stood about 35 yards tall)
67 i.e., it is God who gives us life, but in time we must give that life back to
    Him
68 i.e., the day when that debt matures and becomes collectible
69 demands (as in calling in a loan)

me? Well, 'tis no matter, honor pricks[70] me on. Yea, but how
130 if honor prick me off when I come on? How then can honor
set to[71] a leg? No, or an arm? No, or take away the grief of a
wound? No, honor hath no skill in surgery,[72] then? No, what
is honor? A word. What is in that word, "honor"? What is that
honor? Air.[73] A trim[74] reckoning. Who hath it? He that died
135 a[75] Wednesday, doth he feel it? No. Doth he hear it? No. 'Tis
insensible,[76] then? Yea, to the dead. But will it not live with
the living. No. Why? Detraction[77] will not suffer it. Therefore
I'll none of it. Honor is a mere scutcheon.[78] And so ends my
catechism.

EXIT

70 (1) pierces, agitates, (2) pushes
71 set to = (1) add (restore), (2) attend to, heal
72 healing, medical practice
73 it is air
74 proper, fine, sound
75 on
76 incapable of being sensed/perceived
77 slander
78 escutcheon = painted representation of a coat of arms

SCENE 2

Shrewsbury, the rebel camp

ENTER WORCESTER AND VERNON

Worcester O no, my nephew must not know, Sir Richard,
    The liberal and kind offer of the King.

Vernon   'Twere best he did.

Worcester   Then are we all undone.
    It is not possible, it cannot be
    The King should keep his word in loving us.   5
    He will suspect us still,[1] and find a time
    To punish this offense in other faults.
    Supposition[2] all our lives shall be stuck full of eyes.
    For treason is but trusted like the fox,
    Who never so tame, so cherished and locked up,   10
    Will have a wild trick[3] of[4] his ancestors,
    Look how he[5] can, or[6] sad or merrily.
    Interpretation will misquote our looks,
    And we shall feed like oxen at a stall,[7]
    The better cherished, still[8] the nearer death.   15
    My nephew's trespass[9] may be well forgot,
    It hath the excuse of youth and heat of blood,

---

1 always
2 assume that
3 (1) stratagem, ruse, wile, (2) trait, custom, practice
4 (1) belonging to, (2) from
5 Folio: he; Quarto: we
6 whether
7 market stand/shop ("butcher shop")
8 always
9 sin

And an adopted[10] name of privilege:[11]
A hair-brained "Hotspur," governed by a spleen.
20 All his offenses live upon my head,
And on his father's. We did train him on,[12]
And his corruption being ta'en[13] from us,
We as the spring[14] of all shall pay for all.
Therefore, good cousin, let not Harry know
25 In any case[15] the offer of the King.

ENTER HOTSPUR

Vernon Deliver what you will, I'll say 'tis so.
Here comes your cousin.

Hotspur   My uncle is returned.
(*to a subordinate*) Deliver up[16] my Lord of Westmoreland.
Uncle, what news?

30 *Worcester* The King will bid you battle presently.
Douglas Defy him by[17] the Lord of Westmoreland.
Hotspur Lord Douglas,[18] go you and tell him[19] so.
Douglas Marry and shall, and very willingly.

EXIT DOUGLAS

---

10 assumed
11 of privilege = with a special advantage
12 train him on = instruct him
13 being ta'en = having been gotten/obtained
14 fountain, source
15 event, circumstance
16 deliver up = free (Westmoreland is the security hostage given to the rebels by the King)
17 by means of
18 either DAHgliss or DOOgeLAS
19 Westmoreland

Worcester There is no seeming[20] mercy in the King.

Hotspur Did you beg any? God forbid.   35

Worcester I told him gently[21] of our grievances,
  Of his oath-breaking, which he mended thus,
  By now forswearing that he is forsworn.[22]
  He calls us rebels, traitors, and will scourge
  With haughty arms this hateful name in us.   40

ENTER DOUGLAS

Douglas Arm, gentlemen, to arms, for I have thrown
  A brave defiance in King Henry's teeth.
  And Westmoreland that was engaged did bear it,
  Which cannot choose[23] but bring him quickly on.[24]

Worcester The Prince of Wales stepped forth before the King   45
  And, nephew, challenged you to single fight.

Hotspur O would[25] the quarrel lay upon our heads,
  And that no man might draw short breath[26] today
  But I and Harry Monmouth.[27] Tell me, tell me,
  How showed his tasking?[28] Seemed it in contempt?   50

Vernon No, by my soul, I never in my life
  Did hear a challenge urged more modestly,[29]

20 (1) apparent, (2) fitting, proper
21 courteously
22 is forsworn = has perjured himself, falsely sworn
23 help
24 bring him quickly on = cause him to advance / attack speedily
25 I wish that
26 draw short breath = pant (breathe rapidly from exertion)
27 Hal
28 demanding, calling to account
29 moderately

Unless[30] a brother should a brother dare
To gentle exercise[31] and proof of arms.
55 He gave[32] you all the duties[33] of a man,
Trimmed[34] up your praises with a princely tongue,
Spoke your deservings like a chronicle,
Making you ever better than his praise
By still dispraising[35] praise, valued[36] with you.
60 And, which became him like a prince indeed,
He made a blushing cital[37] of himself,
And chid his truant youth with such a grace
As if he mastered there a double spirit[38]
Of teaching and of learning instantly.[39]
65 There did he pause. But let me tell the world,
If he outlive the envy[40] of this day,
England did never owe[41] so sweet a hope
So much misconstrued in his wantonness.

Hotspur Cousin, I think thou art enamored
70   On[42] his follies. Never did I hear
Of[43] any prince so wild a liberty.[44]

30 except if
31 practice, performance
32 granted, awarded
33 respect, deference
34 dressed, supplied, decorated
35 still dispraising = always disparaging/disapproving of
36 if appraised in comparison
37 citation
38 character, disposition
39 at that very moment, at once ("simultaneously")
40 hostilities
41 possess, own
42 of
43 concerning, about
44 wild a liberty = uncivilized/barbarous a licentiousness/lack of restraint

But be he as he will, yet once ere night
I will embrace[45] him with a soldier's arm,[46]
That[47] he shall shrink under my courtesy.
Arm, arm with speed! And fellows, soldiers, friends,   75
Better[48] consider what you have to do
Than I, that have not well the gift of tongue,
Can lift your blood up with persuasion.[49]

ENTER A MESSENGER

Messenger My lord, here are letters for you.
Hotspur   I cannot read them now.   80
     O gentlemen, the time of life is short.
     To spend that shortness basely were too long.
     If life did ride upon a dial's point,
     Still[50] ending at the arrival of an[51] hour,
     And if we live, we live to tread on kings,   85
     If die, brave[52] death when princes die with us.
     Now, for our consciences, the arms are fair
     When the intent of bearing them is just.

ENTER ANOTHER MESSENGER

Messenger My lord, prepare, the King comes on apace.[53]
Hotspur   I thank him that he cuts me from my tale,   90

45 greet
46 weapon
47 so that
48 it is better that you
49 arguments, entreaties
50 always
51 a certain / definite / fixed
52 (verb) then challenge / defy
53 quickly, rapidly

For I profess not[54] talking. Only this,
Let each man do his best. And here draw I a sword,
Whose temper[55] I intend to stain
With the best blood that I can meet withal
95   In the adventure of this perilous day.
Now Esperance, Percy! And set on,[56]
Sound all the lofty instruments of war,
And by that music let us all embrace,
For, heaven to earth,[57] some of us never shall
100   A second time do[58] such a courtesy.

THEY EMBRACE. THE TRUMPETS SOUND

EXEUNT

54 profess not = don't claim skill at
55 condition, balance
56 set on = attack
57 i.e., as surely as heaven is greater than earth
58 perform

SCENE 3

The battlefield

ENTER DOUGLAS AND BLUNT (DISGUISED AS THE KING)

Blunt   What is thy name, that in battle thus
    Thou crossest[1] me? What honor dost thou seek
    Upon my head?
Douglas   Know then my name is Douglas,
    And I do haunt thee in the battle thus
    Because some tell me that thou art a king.   5
Blunt   They tell thee true.
Douglas The Lord of Stafford dear today hath bought[2]
    Thy likeness, for instead of thee, King Harry,
    This sword hath ended him, so shall it thee
    Unless thou yield[3] thee as my prisoner.   10
Blunt   I was not born a yielder, thou proud Scot,
    And thou shalt find a king that will revenge
    Lord Stafford's death.

THEY FIGHT. DOUGLAS KILLS BLUNT

ENTER HOTSPUR

Hotspur O Douglas, hadst thou fought at Holmedon thus
    I never had triumphèd upon a Scot.   15
Douglas All's done, all's won, here breathless[4] lies the King.
Hotspur Where?
Douglas Here.

1 (1) encounter, face, (2) obstruct
2 (1) acquired, purchased, (2) paid the penalty for having
3 hand over, surrender
4 lifeless, dead

Hotspur This, Douglas? No, I know this face full well.

20   A gallant knight he was, his name was Blunt,

Semblably⁵ furnished like the King himself.

Douglas (*to corpse*) Ah fool, go with thy soul whither it goes.

A borrowed title hast thou bought too dear.

Why didst thou tell me that thou wert a king?

25 *Hotspur* The King hath many marching in his coats.⁶

Douglas Now by my sword, I will kill all his coats.

I'll murder all his wardrobe, piece by piece,

Until I meet the King.

Hotspur   Up and away!

Our soldiers stand full fairly⁷ for the day.⁸

EXEUNT

ALARUM⁹

ENTER FALSTAFF

30 *Falstaff* Though I could scape shot-free¹⁰ at London, I fear the
shot here. Here's no scoring but upon the pate. (*to Blunt's
corpse*) Soft, who are you? Sir Walter Blunt. There's honor for
you! Here's no vanity. I am as hot as molten lead, and as heavy
too. God keep lead out of me. I need no more weight than

35   mine own bowels. I have led my ragamuffins where they are
peppered. There's not three of my hundred and fifty left alive,

---

5 deceptively (semBLAbly)
6 mail coats, suits of armor
7 are favorably situated, have a very good chance
8 for the day = for the result/outcome of the day's combat
9 call to battle
10 (1) free from payment of bills ("scot free"), (2) free from being shot

and they are for[11] the town's end, to beg during life.[12] But
who comes here?

ENTER HAL

Hal   What, stands thou idle here? Lend me thy sword.
          Many a noble man lies stark[13] and stiff,   40
          Under the hoofs of vaunting[14] enemies,
          Whose[15] deaths are yet unrevenged. I prithee,
          Lend me thy sword.
Falstaff O Hal, I prithee give me leave to breathe awhile. Turk[16]
          Gregory[17] never did such deeds in arms as I have done this   45
          day. I have paid Percy, I have made him sure.[18]
Hal   He is indeed, and living to kill thee.
          I prithee, lend me thy sword.
Falstaff Nay, before God, Hal, if Percy be alive thou gets not my
          sword, but take my pistol if thou wilt.   50
Hal   Give it me. What, is it in the case?[19]
Falstaff Ay Hal, 'tis hot, 'tis hot. There's that will sack[20] a city.

HAL DRAWS IT OUT, AND FINDS IT TO BE A BOTTLE OF SACK

Hal   What, is it a time to jest and dally[21] now?

11 are for = have gone to
12 during life = while still alive
13 rigid, hard
14 boasting
15 men whose
16 barbarian, savage
17 unidentified
18 made him sure = (1) ruined/killed him for sure/certainly, *or* (2) rendered
   him safe/free from risk (to us)
19 holder, holster
20 plunder, despoil
21 play, fool about

HAL THROWS THE BOTTLE AT FALSTAFF

EXIT HAL

Falstaff Well, if Percy be alive, I'll pierce him. If he do come in
my way (*thrusting his sword*), so. If he do not, if I come in his
willingly, let him make a carbonado[22] of me. I like not such
grinning honor as Sir Walter hath. Give me life, which if I can
save, so.[23] If not, honor comes unlooked for, and there's an
end.

EXIT

22 meat scored/slashed across and then grilled
23 so be it

SCENE 4

The battlefield

ALARUMS. EXCURSIONS[1]

ENTER THE KING, HAL, LORD JOHN OF LANCASTER,
EARL OF WESTMORELAND

King   I prithee, Harry, withdraw thyself, thou bleedest
too much.

Lord John of Lancaster, go you with him.

John   Not I, my lord, unless I did bleed too.

Hal   I beseech your Majesty, make up,[2]

Lest your retirement do amaze[3] your friends.   5

King   I will do so. My Lord of Westmoreland,

Lead him to his tent.

Westmoreland (*to Hal*) Come, my lord, I'll lead you to your tent.

Hal   Lead me, my lord? I do not need your help,

And God forbid a shallow scratch should drive   10

The Prince of Wales from such a field as this,

Where stained nobility lies trodden on,

And rebels' arms triumph in massacres.[4]

John   We breathe[5] too long. Come, cousin
Westmoreland,

Our duty this way lies. For God's sake, come.   15

EXEUNT JOHN AND WESTMORELAND

---

1 soldiers running in and out
2 make up = come forward, advance
3 (1) bewilder, perplex, overwhelm, (2) stun, (3) alarm, terrify
4 general slaughter
5 rest

Hal   By God, thou hast deceived me, Lancaster,

I did not think thee lord[6] of such a spirit.

Before I loved thee as a brother, John,

But now I do respect thee as[7] my soul.

20 *King*   I saw him hold Lord Percy at the point,[8]

With lustier maintenance[9] than I did look for

Of such an ungrown[10] warrior.

Hal   O, this boy lends mettle to us all.

EXIT HAL

ENTER DOUGLAS

Douglas Another king? They grow like Hydra's heads.[11]

25 I am the Douglas, fatal to all those

That wear those colors on them. What art thou

That counterfeit'st the person of a king?

King   The King himself, who, Douglas, grieves at heart

So many[12] of his shadows thou hast met

30 And not the very King. I have two boys

Seek[13] Percy and thyself about the field.

But seeing thou fall'st on[14] me so luckily

I will assay[15] thee. So, defend thyself.

---

6 master

7 as I do

8 at the point = at sword point

9 lustier maintenance = more vigorous performance/behavior

10 immature

11 Hydra's heads: nine-headed mythical monster who grew back two heads for
every one cut off

12 so many = that so many

13 who seek

14 fall'st on = come/happen upon

15 test, try

Douglas I fear thou art another counterfeit,

    And yet in faith thou bear'st thee like a king. 35

    But mine I am sure thou art, whoe'er thou be,

    And thus I win thee.

          THEY FIGHT; THE KING IS IN DANGER

                ENTER HAL

Hal   Hold up thy head,[16] vile Scot, or thou art like

    Never to hold it up again. The spirits

    Of valiant Shirley, Stafford, Blunt are in my arms. 40

    It is the Prince of Wales that threatens thee,

    Who never promiseth but he means to pay.

          THEY FIGHT. DOUGLAS FLEES

    (*to King*) Cheerly,[17] my lord. How fares your grace?

    Sir Nicholas Gawsey hath for succor[18] sent,

    And so hath Clifton. I'll to Clifton straight. 45

King   Stay and breathe a while.

    Thou hast redeemed thy lost opinion,[19]

    And showed thou makst some tender[20] of my life,

    In this fair rescue thou hast brought to me.

Hal   O God, they did me too much injury, 50

    That ever said I hearkened for[21] your death.

    If it were so, I might have let alone

    The insulting[22] hand of Douglas over you,

16 hold up thy head = maintain/preserve your dignity
17 heartily
18 assistance, aid
19 owPIneeOWN
20 regard, concern
21 hearkened for = sought
22 triumphantly scornful/contemptuous

Which would have been as speedy in your end

55 As all the poisonous potions in the world,

And saved the treacherous labor of your son.

King   Make up to[23] Clifton, I'll to Sir Nicholas Gawsey.

EXIT KING

ENTER HOTSPUR

Hotspur   If I mistake not, thou art Harry Monmouth.

Hal   Thou speakst as if I would deny my name.

Hotspur   My name is Harry Percy.

60 *Hal*   Why then I see

A very valiant rebel of the name.

I am the Prince of Wales, and think not, Percy,

To share with me in glory any more.

Two stars keep[24] not their motion in one sphere,[25]

65 Nor can one England brook a double reign

Of Harry Percy and the Prince of Wales.

Hotspur   Nor shall it, Harry, for the hour is come

To end the one of us, and would to God

Thy name in arms were now as great as mine![26]

70 *Hal*   I'll make it[27] greater ere I part from thee,

And all the budding honors on thy crest

I'll crop[28] to make a garland for my head.

Hotspur   I can no longer brook thy vanities.

---

23 make up to = (1) supply, (2) go to

24 hold, maintain

25 (1) Ptolemaic sphere, one star for each sphere, (2) orbit

26 i.e., if Hal had a higher reputation, defeating him would be more glorious

27 my reputation

28 remove, cut off

THEY FIGHT

ENTER FALSTAFF

Falstaff Well said, Hal, to it, Hal. Nay, you shall find no boys'
  play here, I can tell you.   75

ENTER DOUGLAS, WHO FIGHTS WITH FALSTAFF

FALSTAFF FALLS DOWN AS IF HE WERE DEAD

EXIT DOUGLAS

HAL KILLS PERCY

Hotspur O Harry, thou hast robbed me of my youth.
  I better brook the loss of brittle life
  Than those proud titles thou hast won of [29] me.
  They wound my thoughts worse than thy sword my flesh.
  But thoughts, the slaves of life, and life, time's fool,   80
  And time, that takes survey[30] of all the world,
  Must have a stop. O I could prophesy,
  But that the earthy and cold hand of death
  Lies on my tongue. No, Percy, thou art dust
  And food for –   85
            HOTSPUR DIES

Hal   For worms, brave Percy. Fare thee well, great heart.
  Ill-weaved[31] ambition, how much art thou shrunk.
  When that this body did contain a spirit,
  A kingdom for it was too small a bound.
  But now two paces of the vilest earth   90

29 from ("off")
30 a commanding/comprehensive view/inspection (sirVEY)
31 ill-weaved = ill-woven/formed

Is room enough. This earth that bears thee dead
Bears not alive so stout[32] a gentleman.
If thou wert sensible of[33] courtesy
I should not make so dear[34] a show of zeal.

95 But let my favors[35] hide thy mangled face,
And even in[36] thy behalf I'll thank my self
For doing these fair rites of tenderness.
Adieu, and take thy praise with thee to heaven.
Thy[37] ignominy[38] sleep with thee in the grave,

100 But not remembered in thy epitaph.

HE SEES FALSTAFF ON THE GROUND

What, old acquaintance, could not all this flesh
Keep in a little life? Poor Jack, farewell.
I could have better spared a better man.
O, I should have a heavy miss[39] of thee,

105 If I were much in love with vanity.
Death hath not struck so fat a deer today,
Though many dearer in this bloody fray.
Embowellèd[40] will I see thee by and by,
Till then, in blood, by noble Percy lie.

EXIT HAL

32 brave, resolute, splendid, proud
33 sensible of = able to feel
34 affectionate, warm
35 i.e., ribbon(s), scarf(ves), etc., which Hal takes off and places on the corpse's
face
36 even in = precisely on
37 may thy
38 dishonor, disgrace (IGnaMInee)
39 loss
40 cutting out of intestines, for embalming

FALSTAFF STANDS UP

Falstaff Embowellèd? If thou embowel me today, I'll give you   110
leave to powder[41] me and eat me too tomorrow. 'Sblood,
'twas time to counterfeit, or that hot termagant[42] Scot had[43]
paid me scot and lot[44] too. Counterfeit? I lie, I am no
counterfeit. To die is to be a counterfeit, for he is but the
counterfeit of a man, who hath not the life of a man. But to   115
counterfeit dying, when a man thereby liveth, is to be no
counterfeit, but the true and perfect image of life indeed. The
better part of valor is discretion,[45] in the which better part I
have saved my life. Zounds, I am afraid of this gunpowder[46]
Percy, though he be dead. How if he should counterfeit too   120
and rise? By my faith, I am afraid he would prove the better
counterfeit. Therefore I'll make him sure, yea, and I'll swear I
killed him. Why may not he rise as well as I? Nothing
confutes me but eyes, and nobody sees me. (*stabbing the corpse*)
Therefore, sirrah, with a new wound in your thigh, come you   125
along with me.

HE PUTS HOTSPUR ON HIS BACK

ENTER HAL AND JOHN OF LANCASTER

Hal   Come, brother John, full bravely hast thou fleshed[47]
Thy maiden[48] sword.

---

41 (1) season, spice, (2) salt, for curing
42 savage/violent bully
43 would have
44 scot and lot = paid out thoroughly (originally, taxes for municipal expenses)
45 judgment
46 fiery, explosive
47 initiated to bloodshed
48 virginal

John   But soft, whom have we here?

     Did you not tell me this fat man was dead?

130 *Hal*   I did, I saw him dead,

     Breathless and bleeding on the ground. Art thou alive?

     Or is it fantasy[49] that plays upon our eyesight?

     I prithee speak, we will not trust our eyes

     Without our ears. Thou art not what thou seemst.

135 *Falstaff* No, that's certain. I am not a double-man.[50] But if I be

     not Jack Falstaff, then am I a Jack. (*throwing the corpse down*)

     There is Percy. If your father will do me any honor, so. If not,

     let him kill the next Percy himself. I look[51] to be either earl

     or duke,[52] I can assure you.

140 *Hal*   Why, Percy I killed myself, and saw thee dead.

     Falstaff Didst thou? Lord, Lord, how this world is given to lying.

     I grant you I was down, and out of breath, and so was he, but

     we rose both at an instant, and fought a long hour by

     Shrewsbury clock.[53] If I may be believed, so. If not, let them

145   that should reward valor bear the sin upon their own heads.

     I'll take it upon my death, I gave him this wound in the thigh.

     If the man were alive, and would deny it, zounds, I would

     make him eat a piece of my sword.

     John   This is the strangest tale that ever I heard.

150 *Hal*   This is the strangest fellow, brother John.

     (*openly, to Falstaff*) Come, bring your luggage[54] nobly on your

     back.

---

49 imagination, hallucination
50 wraith, phantom
51 expect
52 either earl or duke = either an earl or a duke
53 i.e., the tolling of public clocks could be heard from a good distance
54 heavy baggage

(*aside, to Falstaff*) For my part, if a lie may do thee grace,
I'll gild[55] it with the happiest[56] terms I have.

A RETREAT IS SOUNDED

Hal　　The trumpet sounds retreat, the day is ours.
Come brother, let us to the highest[57] of the field,　　　　155
To see what friends are living, who are dead.

EXEUNT HAL AND JOHN

Falstaff　I'll follow, as they say, for reward.[58] He that rewards me,
God reward him. If I do grow great,[59] I'll grow less,[60] for I'll
purge[61] and leave sack, and live cleanly[62] as a nobleman
should do.　　　　160

EXIT

55 adorn (cover over with a thin layer of gold)
56 most favorable
57 highest part
58 my remuneration/recompense
59 of high rank
60 thinner
61 get rid of whatever is extraneous
62 chastely, innocently, purely

SCENE 5

The battlefield

TRUMPETS SOUND

ENTER THE KING, HAL, JOHN, WESTMORELAND,
WITH WORCESTER AND VERNON AS PRISONERS

King Thus ever did rebellion find rebuke.
Ill-spirited[1] Worcester, did not we send grace,
Pardon, and terms of love to all of you?
And wouldst thou turn our offers contrary?[2]

5 Misuse the tenor of thy kinsman's trust?
Three knights upon[3] our party slain today,
A noble earl and many a creature else,
Had been alive this hour,
If like a Christian thou hadst truly borne

10 Betwixt our armies true intelligence.[4]

Worcester What I have done my safety urged me to.
And I embrace this fortune patiently,
Since not to be avoided it falls on me.

King Bear Worcester to the death, and Vernon too.

15 Other offenders we will pause upon.

EXEUNT WORCESTER AND VERNON, GUARDED

How goes the field?

Hal The noble Scot, Lord Douglas, when he saw
The fortune of the day quite turned from him,

---

1 ill-spirited = evil-disposed/inclined
2 in the opposite direction, diametrically different
3 within, in
4 knowledge, information

The noble Percy slain and all his men
Upon the foot of⁵ fear, fled with the rest. 20
And falling from a hill, he was so bruised⁶
That the pursuers took him. At my tent
The Douglas is, and I beseech your grace
I may dispose of⁷ him.

King   With all my heart.

Hal   Then brother John of Lancaster, 25
To you this honorable bounty⁸ shall belong.
Go to the Douglas and deliver him
Up to his pleasure, ransomless and free.
His valors shown upon our crests today
Have taught us how to cherish such high deeds, 30
Even in the bosom of our adversaries.

John   I thank your grace for this high courtesy,
Which I shall give away⁹ immediately.

King   Then this remains, that we divide our power.
You, son John, and my cousin Westmoreland 35
Towards York shall bend, you with your dearest¹⁰ speed,
To meet Northumberland and the Prelate Scroop,
Who (as we hear) are busily in arms.
Myself and you, son Harry, will towards Wales,
To fight with Glendower and the Earl of March.¹¹ 40

---

5 upon the foot of = running in
6 Holinshed says he injured a testicle (Raphael Holinshed, *Chronicles of England, Scotland, and Ireland*, 1577)
7 dispose of = make arrangements for, deal with
8 goodness, virtue, kindness, graciousness
9 give away = dispose of, set into full operation
10 best
11 Mortimer

Rebellion in this land shall lose his sway,
Meeting the check[12] of such another day,
And since this business[13] so fair is done,
Let us not leave till all our own be won.

EXEUNT

12 defeat (from "check" in the popular war game, chess)
13 BIziNESS

Falstaff is to the world of the histories what Shylock is to the comedies and Hamlet to the tragedies: *the* problematical representation. Falstaff, Shylock, Hamlet put to us the question: precisely how does Shakespearean representation differ from anything before it, and how has it overdetermined our expectations of representation ever since?

The fortunes of Falstaff in scholarship and criticism have been endlessly dismal, and I will not resume them here. I prefer Harold Goddard on Falstaff to any other commentator, and yet I am aware that Goddard appears to have sentimentalized and even idealized Falstaff. I would say better that than the endless litany absurdly patronizing Falstaff as Vice, Parasite, Fool, Braggart Soldier, Corrupt Glutton, Seducer of Youth, Cowardly Liar, and everything else that would not earn the greatest wit in all literature an honorary degree at Yale or a place on the board of the Ford Foundation.

Falstaff, I will venture, in Shakespeare rather than in Verdi, is precisely what Nietzsche tragically attempted yet failed to represent in his Zarathustra: a person without a superego, or should I say, Socrates without the *daimon*. Perhaps even better, Falstaff is not the Sancho Panza of Cervantes, but the exemplary figure of Kafka's parable "The Truth about Sancho Panza." Kafka's Sancho Panza, a free man, has diverted his daimon from him by many nightly feedings of chivalric romances (it would be science fiction nowadays). Diverted from Sancho, his true object, the daimon becomes the harmless Don Quixote, whose mishaps prove edifying entertainment for the "philosophic" Sancho, who proceeds to follow his errant daimon, out of a sense of responsibility. Falstaff's "failure," if it can be termed that, is that he fell in love, not with his own daimon, but with his bad son, Hal, who all too truly is Bolingbroke's son. The witty knight should have diverted his own daimon with Shakespearean comedies, and philosophically have followed the daimon off to the forest of Arden.

Falstaff is neither good enough nor bad enough to flourish in the world of the histories. But then he is necessarily beyond, not only good and evil, but cause and effect as well. A greater monist than the young Milton, Falstaff plays at dualism partly in order to mock all dualisms, whether Christian, Platonic, or even the Freudian dualism that he both anticipates and in some sense refutes.

Falstaff provoked the best of all critics, Dr. Johnson, into the judgment that "he has nothing in him that can be esteemed." George Bernard Shaw, perhaps out of envy, called Falstaff "a besotted and disgusting old wretch." Yet Falstaff's sole rival in Shakespeare is Hamlet; no one else, as Oscar Wilde noted, has so comprehensive a consciousness. Representation itself changed permanently because of Hamlet and Falstaff. I begin with my personal favorite among all of Falstaff's remarks, if only because I plagiarize it daily:

O, thou has damnable iteration, and art indeed able to
corrupt a saint. Thou hast done much harm upon me,
Hal, God forgive thee for it. Before I knew thee, Hal, I
knew nothing, and now am I, if a man should speak truly,
little better than one of the wicked. [1.2.81–85]

W. H. Auden, whose Falstaff essentially was Verdi's, believed
the knight to be "a comic symbol for the supernatural order of
charity" and thus a displacement of Christ into the world of wit.
The charm of this reading, though considerable, neglects Falstaff's grandest quality, his immanence. He is as immanent a representation as Hamlet is transcendent. Better than any formula-
tion of Freud's, Falstaff perpetually shows us that the ego indeed is
always a bodily ego. And the bodily ego is always vulnerable, and
Hal indeed has done much harm upon it, and will do far worse,
and will need forgiveness, though no sensitive audience ever will
forgive him. Falstaff, like Hamlet, and like Lear's Fool, does speak
truly, and Falstaff remains, despite Hal, rather better than one of
the wicked, or the good.

For what is supreme immanence in what might be called the
order of representation? This is another way of asking: is not Falstaff, like Hamlet, so original a representation that he originates
much of what we know or expect about representation? We cannot see how original Falstaff is because Falstaff *contains* us; we do
not contain him. And though we love Falstaff, he does not need
our love any more than Hamlet does. His sorrow is that he loves
Hal rather more than Hamlet loves Ophelia, or even Gertrude.
The Hamlet of act 5 is past loving anyone, but that is a gift (if it is
a gift) resulting from transcendence. If you dwell wholly in this

world, and if you are, as Falstaff is, a *pervasive* entity, or as Freud would say, "a strong egoism," then you must begin to love, as Freud also says, in order that you may not fall ill. But what if your strong eoism is not afflicted by any ego-ideal, what if you are never watched, or watched over, by what is above the ego? Falstaff is *not* subject to a power that watches, discovers, and criticizes all his intentions. Falstaff, except for his single and misplaced love, is free, is freedom itself, because he seems free of the superego.

Why does Falstaff (and not his parody in *The Merry Wives of Windsor*) pervade histories rather than comedies? To begin is to be free, and you cannot begin freshly in comedy any more than you can in tragedy. Both genres are family romances, at least in Shakespeare. History in Shakespeare is hardly the genre of freedom for kings and nobles, but it is for Falstaff. How and why? Falstaff is of course his own mother and his own father, begotten out of wit by caprice. Ideally he wants nothing except the audience, which he always has; who could watch anyone else on stage when Ralph Richardson was playing Falstaff? Not so ideally, he evidently wants the love of a son, and invests in Hal, the impossible object. But primarily he has what he must have, the audience's fascination with the ultimate image of freedom. His precursor in Shakespeare is not Puck or Bottom, but Faulconbridge the Bastard in *The Life and Death of King John*. Each has a way of providing a daemonic chorus that renders silly all royal and noble squabbles and intrigues. The Bastard in *John,* forthright like his father Richard the Lion Heart, is not a wicked wit, but his truth-telling brutally prophesies Falstaff's function.

There are very nearly as many Falstaffs as there are critics, which probably is as it should be. These proliferating Falstaffs tend either to be degraded or idealized, again perhaps inevitably. One of the most ambiguous Falstaffs was created by the late Sir William Empson: "He is the scandalous upper-class man whose behavior embarrasses his class and thereby pleases the lower class in the audience, as an 'exposure.'" To Empson, Falstaff also was both nationalist and Machiavel, "and he had a dangerous amount of power." Empson shared the hint of Wyndham Lewis that Falstaff was homosexual, and so presumably lusted (doubtless in vain) after Hal. To complete this portrait, Empson added that Falstaff, being both an aristocrat and a mob leader, was "a familiar dangerous type," a sort of Alcibiades one presumes.

Confronted by so ambiguous a Falstaff, I return to the sublime knight's rhetoric, which I read very differently, since Falstaff's power seems to me not at all a matter of class, sexuality, politics, or nationalism. Power it is: sublime pathos, *potentia,* the drive for life, more life, at every and any cost. I will propose that Falstaff is neither a noble synecdoche nor a grand hyperbole, but rather a metalepsis or far-fetcher, to use Puttenham's term. To exist without a superego is to be a solar trajectory, an ever-early brightness, which Nietzsche's Zarathustra, in his bathos, failed to be. "Try to live as though it were morning," Nietzsche advises. Falstaff does not need the advice, as we discover when we first encounter him:

Falstaff   Now, Hal, what time of day is it, lad?

Hal   Thou art so fat-witted with drinking of old sack, and
     unbuttoning thee after supper, and sleeping upon benches
     after noon, that thou hast forgotten to demand that truly
     which thou wouldst truly know. What a divel hast thou to do
     with the time of the day? Unless hours were cups of sack, and
     minutes capons, and clocks the tongues of bawds, and dials

the signs of leaping-houses, and the blessèd sun himself a fair hot wench in flame-colored taffeta, I see no reason why thou shouldst be so superfluous, to demand the time of the day.
[1.2.1–11]

I take it that wit here remains with Falstaff, who is not only witty in himself but the cause of wit in his ephebe, Prince Hal, who mocks his teacher, but in the teacher's own exuberant manner and mode. Perhaps there is a double meaning when Falstaff opens his reply with: "Indeed you come near me now Hal," since near is as close as the Prince is capable of, when he imitates the master. Master of what? is the crucial question, generally answered so badly. To take up the stance of most Shakespeare scholars is to associate Falstaff with "such inordinate and low desires, / Such poor, such bare, such lewd, such mean attempts, / Such barren pleasures, rude society." I quote King Henry the Fourth, aggrieved usurper, whose description of Falstaff's aura is hardly recognizable to the audience. We recognize rather: "Counterfeit? I lie, I am no counterfeit. To die is to be a counterfeit, for he is but the counterfeit of a man who hath not the life of a man; but to counterfeit dying, when a man thereby liveth, is to be no counterfeit, but the true and perfect image of life indeed." As Falstaff rightly says, he has saved his life by counterfeiting death, and presumably the moralizing critics would be delighted had the unrespectable knight been butchered by Douglas, "that hot termagant Scot."

The true and perfect image of life, Falstaff, confirms his truth and perfection by counterfeiting dying and so evading death. Though he is given to parodying Puritan preachers, Falstaff has an authentic obsession with the dreadful parable of the rich man and

Lazarus in Luke 16:19 ff. A certain rich man, a purple-clad glutton, is contrasted with the beggar Lazarus, who desired "to be fed with the crumbs which fell from the rich man's table: moreover the dogs came and licked his sores." Both glutton and beggar die, but Lazarus is carried into Abraham's bosom, and the purple glutton into hell, from which he cries vainly for Lazarus to come and cool his tongue. Falstaff stares at Bardolph, his Knight of the Burning Lamp, and affirms: "I never see thy face but I think upon hell-fire, and Dives that lived in purple; for there he is in his robes, burning, burning." Confronting his hundred and fifty tattered prodigals, as he marches them off to be food for powder, Falstaff calls them "slaves as ragged as Lazarus in the painted cloth, where the glutton's dogs licked his sores." In *Henry IV, Part 2,* Falstaff's first speech again returns to this fearful text, as he cries out against one who denies him credit: "Let him be damned like the glutton! Pray God his tongue be hotter!" Despite the ironies abounding in Falstaff the glutton invoking Dives, Shakespeare reverses the New Testament, and Falstaff ends, like Lazarus, in Abraham's bosom, according to the convincing testimony of Mistress Quickly in *Henry V,* where Arthur Britishly replaces Abraham:

Bardolph   Would I were with him, wheresome'er he is, either in
   heaven or in hell!
Hostess   Nay sure, he's not in hell; he's in Arthur's bosom, if ever
   man went to Arthur's bosom. 'A made a finer end, and went
   away and it had been any christom child.

In dying, Falstaff is a newly baptized child, innocent of all stain. The pattern of allusions to Luke suggests a crossing over, with the rejected Falstaff a poor Lazarus upon his knees in front of Dives wearing the royal purple of Henry V. To a moralizing critic this is outrageous, but Shakespeare does stranger tricks with biblical texts. Juxtapose the two moments:

Falstaff My King, my Jove! I speak to thee, my heart!
King   I know thee not, old man, fall to thy prayers.
    How ill white hairs becomes a fool and jester!
    I have long dreamt of such a kind of man,
    So surfeit-swell'd, so old, and so profane;
    But being awak'd, I do despise my dream.

And here is Abraham, refusing to let Lazarus come to comfort the "clothed in purple" Dives: "And beside all this, between us and you there is a great gulf fixed: so that they which would pass from hence to you cannot; neither can they pass to us, that would come from thence."

Wherever Henry V is, he is not in Arthur's bosom, with the rejected Falstaff.

I suggest that Shakespearean representation in the histories indeed demands our understanding of what Shakespeare did to history, in contrast to what his contemporaries did. Standard scholarly views of literary history, and all Marxist reductions of literature and history alike, have the curious allied trait of working very well for, say, Thomas Dekker, but being absurdly irrelevant for Shakespeare. Falstaff and the Tudor theory of kingship? Falstaff and surplus value? I would prefer Falstaff and Nietzsche's vision of the use and abuse of history for life, if it were not that Falstaff triumphs precisely where the Overman fails. One can read Freud on our discomfort in culture backwards, and get somewhere close to Falstaff, but the problem again is that Falstaff triumphs precisely where Freud denies that triumph is possible.

With Falstaff as with Hamlet (and, perhaps, with Cleopatra) Shakespearean representation is so self-begotten and so influential that we can apprehend it only by seeing that it originates us. We cannot judge a mode of representation that has overdetermined our ideas of representation. Like only a few other authors—the Yahwist, Chaucer, Cervantes, Tolstoy—Shakespeare calls recent critiques of literary representation severely into doubt. Jacob, the Pardoner, Sancho Panza, Hadji Murad: it seems absurd to call them figures of rhetoric, let alone to see Falstaff, Hamlet, Shylock, Cleopatra as tropes of ethos and/or of pathos. Falstaff is not language but diction, the product of Shakespeare's will over language, a will that changes characters through and by what they say. Most simply, Falstaff is not how meaning is renewed, but rather how meaning gets started.

Falstaff is so profoundly original a representation because most truly he represents the essence of invention, which is the essence of poetry. He is a perpetual catastrophe, a continuous transference, a universal family romance. If Hamlet is beyond us and beyond our need of him, so that we require our introjection of Horatio, so as to identify ourselves with Horatio's love for Hamlet, then Falstaff too is beyond us. But in the Falstaffian beyonding, as it were, in what I think we must call the Falstaffian sublimity, we are never permitted by Shakespeare to identify ourselves with the Prince's ambivalent affection for Falstaff. Future monarchs have no friends, only followers, and Falstaff, the man without a superego, is no one's follower. Freud never speculated as to what a person without a superego would be like, perhaps because that had been the dangerous prophecy of Nietzsche's Zarathustra. Is there not some sense in which Falstaff's whole being implicitly says to us: "The wisest among you is also merely a conflict and a hybrid between plant and phantom. But do I bid you become phantoms or plants?" Historical critics who call Falstaff a phantom, and moral critics who judge Falstaff to be a plant, can be left to be answered by Sir John himself. Even in his debased form, in *The Merry Wives of Windsor,* he crushes them thus:

> Have I liv'd to stand at the taunt of one that makes fritters of English? This is enough to be the decay of lust and late-walking through the realm.

But most of all Falstaff is a reproach to all critics who seek to demystify mimesis, whether by Marxist or deconstructionist dialectics. Like Hamlet, Falstaff is a super-mimesis, and so compels us to see aspects of reality we otherwise could never apprehend. Marx would teach us what he calls "the appropriation of human reality" and so the appropriation also of human suffering. Nietzsche and his deconstructionist descendants would teach us the necessary irony of failure in every attempt to represent human reality. Falstaff, being more of an original, teaches us himself: "No, that's certain, I am not a double man; but if I be not Jack Falstaff, then am I a Jack." A double man is either a phantom or two men, and a man who is two men might as well be a plant. Sir John is Jack Falstaff; it is the Prince who is a Jack or rascal, and so are Falstaff's moralizing critics. We are in no position then to judge Falstaff or to assess him as a representation of reality. Hamlet is too dispassionate even to *want* to contain us. Falstaff is passionate and challenges us not to bore him, if he is to deign to represent us.

FURTHER READING

This is not a bibliography but a selective set of starting places.

Texts

Hinman, Charlton. *The First Folio of Shakespeare.* 2d ed. Introduction by Peter W. M. Blayney. New York: W. W. Norton, 1996.

Shakespeare, William. *1 Henry IV,* 1598 Quarto. Internet Shakespeare Editions, 10 Nov. 2003.

Language

Dobson, E. J. *English Pronunciation, 1500–1700.* 2d ed. Oxford: Oxford University Press, 1968.

Houston, John Porter. *The Rhetoric of Poetry in the Renaissance and Seventeenth Century.* Baton Rouge: Louisiana State University Press, 1983.

———. *Shakespearean Sentences: A Study in Style and Syntax.* Baton Rouge: Louisiana State University Press, 1988.

Kermode, Frank. *Shakespeare's Language.* New York: Farrar, Straus and Giroux, 2000.

Kökeritz, Helge. *Shakespeare's Pronunciation.* New Haven: Yale University Press, 1953.

Lanham, Richard A. *The Motives of Eloquence: Literary Rhetoric in the Renaissance.* New Haven and London: Yale University Press, 1976.

The Oxford English Dictionary: Second Edition on CD-ROM, version 3.0.
New York: Oxford University Press, 2002.

Raffel, Burton. *From Stress to Stress: An Autobiography of English Prosody*.
Hamden, Conn.: Archon Books, 1992.

Ronberg, Gert. *A Way with Words: The Language of English Renaissance
Literature*. London: Arnold, 1992.

Trousdale, Marion. *Shakespeare and the Rhetoricians*. Chapel Hill:
University of North Carolina Press, 1982.

Culture

Bindoff, S. T. *Tudor England*. Baltimore: Penguin, 1950.

Bradbrook, M. C. *Shakespeare: The Poet in His World*. New York:
Columbia University Press, 1978.

Brown, Cedric C., ed. *Patronage, Politics, and Literary Tradition in England,
1558–1658*. Detroit, Mich.: Wayne State University Press, 1993.

Buxton, John. *Elizabethan Taste*. London: Harvester, 1963.

Cowan, Alexander. *Urban Europe, 1500–1700*. New York: Oxford
University Press, 1998.

Driver, Tom E. *The Sense of History in Greek and Shakespearean Drama*.
New York: Columbia University Press, 1960.

Finucci, Valeria, and Regina Schwartz, eds. *Desire in the Renaissance:
Psychoanalysis and Literature*. Princeton, N.J.: Princeton University
Press, 1994.

Fumerton, Patricia, and Simon Hunt, eds. *Renaissance Culture and the
Everyday*. Philadelphia: University of Pennsylvania Press, 1999.

Halliday, F. E. *Shakespeare in His Age*. South Brunswick, N.J.: Yoseloff,
1965.

Harrison, G. B., ed. *The Elizabethan Journals: Being a Record of Those
Things Most Talked of During the Years 1591–1597*. Abridged ed. 2 vols.
New York: Doubleday Anchor, 1965.

Harrison, William. *The Description of England: The Classic Contemporary
[1577] Account of Tudor Social Life*. Edited by Georges Edelen.
Washington, D.C.: Folger Shakespeare Library, 1968. Reprint, New
York: Dover, 1994.

Jardine, Lisa. "Introduction." In Jardine, *Reading Shakespeare Historically*.
London: Routledge, 1996.

————. *Worldly Goods: A New History of the Renaissance.* London: Macmillan, 1996.

Jeanneret, Michel. *A Feast of Words: Banquets and Table Talk in the Renaissance.* Translated by Jeremy Whiteley and Emma Hughes. Chicago: University of Chicago Press, 1991.

Kernan, Alvin. *Shakespeare, the King's Playwright: Theater in the Stuart Court, 1603–1613.* New Haven: Yale University Press, 1995.

Lockyer, Roger. *Tudor and Stuart Britain, 1471–1714.* London: Longmans, 1964.

Norwich, John Julius. *Shakespeare's Kings: The Great Plays and the History of England in the Middle Ages, 1337–1485.* New York: Scribner, 2000.

Rose, Mary Beth, ed. *Renaissance Drama as Cultural History: Essays from Renaissance Drama, 1977–1987.* Evanston, Ill.: Northwestern University Press, 1990.

Schmidgall, Gary. *Shakespeare and the Courtly Aesthetic.* Berkeley: University of California Press, 1981.

Tillyard, E. M. W. *The Elizabethan World Picture.* London: Chatto and Windus, 1943. Reprint, Harmondsworth: Penguin, 1963.

Willey, Basil. *The Seventeenth Century Background: Studies in the Thought of the Age in Relation to Poetry and Religion.* New York: Columbia University Press, 1933. Reprint, New York: Doubleday, 1955.

Wilson, F. P. *The Plague in Shakespeare's London.* 2d ed. Oxford: Oxford University Press, 1963.

Wilson, John Dover. *Life in Shakespeare's England: A Book of Elizabethan Prose.* 2d ed. Cambridge: Cambridge University Press, 1913. Reprint, Harmondsworth: Penguin, 1944.

Zimmerman, Susan, and Ronald F. E. Weissman, eds. *Urban Life in the Renaissance.* Newark: University of Delaware Press, 1989.

Dramatic Development

Cohen, Walter. *Drama of a Nation: Public Theater in Renaissance England and Spain.* Ithaca, N.Y.: Cornell University Press, 1985.

Dessen, Alan C. *Shakespeare and the Late Moral Plays.* Lincoln: University of Nebraska Press, 1986.

Fraser, Russell A., and Norman Rabkin, eds. *Drama of the English Renaissance.* 2 vols. Upper Saddle River, N.J.: Prentice Hall, 1976.

Happé, Peter, ed. *Tudor Interludes.* Harmondsworth: Penguin, 1972.

Laroque, François. *Shakespeare's Festive World: Elizabethan Seasonal Entertainment and the Professional Stage.* Translated by Janet Lloyd. Cambridge: Cambridge University Press, 1991.

Norland, Howard B. *Drama in Early Tudor Britain, 1485–1558.* Lincoln: University of Nebraska Press, 1995.

Theater and Stage

Doran, Madeleine. *Endeavors of Art: A Study of Form in Elizabethan Drama.* Milwaukee: University of Wisconsin Press, 1954.

Gurr, Andrew. *Playgoing in Shakespeare's London.* Cambridge: Cambridge University Press, 1987.

———. *The Shakespearian Stage, 1574–1642.* 3d ed. Cambridge: Cambridge University Press, 1992.

Harrison, G. B. *Elizabethan Plays and Players.* Ann Arbor: University of Michigan Press, 1956.

Holmes, Martin. *Shakespeare and His Players.* New York: Scribner, 1972.

Ingram, William. *The Business of Playing: The Beginnings of the Adult Professional Theater in Elizabethan London.* Ithaca, N.Y.: Cornell University Press, 1992.

Marcus, Leah S. *Unediting the Renaissance: Shakespeare, Marlowe, Milton.* London: Routledge, 1996.

Orgel, Stephen. *The Authentic Shakespeare, and Other Problems of the Early Modern Stage.* New York: Routledge, 2002.

Salgado, Gamini. *Eyewitnesses of Shakespeare: First Hand Accounts of Performances, 1590–1890.* New York: Barnes and Noble, 1975.

Stern, Tiffany. *Rehearsal from Shakespeare to Sheridan.* Oxford: Clarendon Press, 2000.

Thomson, Peter. *Shakespeare's Professional Career.* Cambridge: Cambridge University Press, 1992.

Weimann, Robert. *Shakespeare and the Popular Tradition in the Theater: Studies in the Social Dimension of Dramatic Form and Function.* Edited by Robert Schwartz. Baltimore: Johns Hopkins University Press, 1978.

Yachnin, Paul. *Stage-Wrights: Shakespeare, Jonson, Middleton, and the*

Making of Theatrical Value. Philadelphia: University of Pennsylvania Press, 1997.

Biography

Halliday, F. E. *The Life of Shakespeare.* Rev. ed. London: Duckworth, 1964.

Honigmann, F. A. J. *Shakespeare: The "Lost Years."* 2d ed. Manchester: Manchester University Press, 1998.

Schoenbaum, Samuel. *Shakespeare's Lives.* New ed. Oxford: Clarendon Press, 1991.

————. *William Shakespeare: A Compact Documentary Life.* Oxford: Oxford University Press, 1977.

General

Bergeron, David M., and Geraldo U. de Sousa. *Shakespeare: A Study and Research Guide.* 3d ed. Lawrence: University of Kansas Press, 1995.

Berryman, John. *Berryman's Shakespeare.* Edited by John Haffenden. Preface by Robert Giroux. New York: Farrar, Straus and Giroux, 1999.

Bradbey, Anne, ed. *Shakespearian Criticism, 1919–35.* London: Oxford University Press, 1936.

Colie, Rosalie L. *Shakespeare's Living Art.* Princeton, N.J.: Princeton University Press, 1974.

Dean, Leonard F., ed. *Shakespeare: Modern Essays in Criticism.* Rev. ed. New York: Oxford University Press, 1967.

Grene, David. *The Actor in History: Studies in Shakespearean Stage Poetry.* University Park: Pennsylvania State University Press, 1988.

Goddard, Harold C. *The Meaning of Shakespeare.* 2 vols. Chicago: University of Chicago Press, 1951.

Kaufmann, Ralph J. *Elizabethan Drama: Modern Essays in Criticism.* New York: Oxford University Press, 1961.

McDonald, Russ. *The Bedford Companion to Shakespeare: An Introduction with Documents.* Boston: Bedford, 1996.

Raffel, Burton. *How to Read a Poem.* New York: Meridian, 1984.

Ricks, Christopher, ed. *English Drama to 1710*. Rev. ed. Harmondsworth: Sphere, 1987.

Siegel, Paul N., ed. *His Infinite Variety: Major Shakespearean Criticism Since Johnson*. Philadelphia: Lippincott, 1964.

Sweeting, Elizabeth J. *Early Tudor Criticism: Linguistic and Literary*. Oxford: Blackwell, 1940.

Van Doren, Mark. *Shakespeare*. New York: Holt, 1939.

Weiss, Theodore. *The Breath of Clowns and Kings: Shakespeare's Early Comedies and Histories*. New York: Atheneum, 1971.

Wells, Stanley, ed. *The Cambridge Companion to Shakespeare Studies*. Cambridge: Cambridge University Press, 1986.

FINDING LIST

Repeated unfamiliar words and meanings, alphabetically arranged, with act, scene, and footnote number of first occurrence, in the spelling (form) of that first occurrence

account		*blood*	1.2.122
(noun)	3.2.107	*bootless*	1.1.40
action	2.3.12	*brave*	1.1.71
advantage	1.1.38	*broils*	1.1.5
adventure	1.1.108	*brooks* (verb)	4.1.56
amendment	1.2.96	*buckler*	1.3.190
an (con-		*buffets*	2.3.19
junction)	1.2.94	*but soft:* see under "soft"	
angel	3.3.76	*by'r lady*	2.4.35
anon	2.1.4	*carriers*	Dram. Pers. 4
apparent	1.2.56	*chamberlain*	Dram. Pers. 3
arms	1.2.148	*charge*	
attend	1.3.175	(noun)	2.4.313
base		*chat* (noun)	1.3.65
(adjective)	1.2.155	*choler*	1.3.110
behalf	1.3.147	*chronicles*	1.3.145